# BRIGHT IDEAS

# Inspirations for POETRY

H M Cart

Published by Scholastic
Publications Ltd,
Villiers House,
Clarendon Avenue,
Leamington Spa,
Warwickshire CV32 5PR

© 1992 Scholastic Publications Ltd

Written by Helen Hadley
Edited by Juliet Gladston
Sub-edited by Catherine Baker
Series designed by Juanita
Puddifoot
Illustrated by Ann Johns (Maggie
Mundy Agency)
Cover design by Clare Brewer
Cover artwork by Ann Johns

Designed using Aldus Pagemaker
Processed by Pages Bureau,
Leamington Spa
Artwork by David Harban Design,
Warwick
Printed in Great Britain by
Ebenezer Baylis & Son, Worcester

**British Library Cataloguing in
Publication Data**
A catalogue record for this book is
available from the British Library.

ISBN 0-590-53009-7

# CONTENTS

# INTRODUCTION

# Poetry

The Bullock Report states that: 'Poetry starts at a disadvantage. In the public view it is something rather odd, certainly outside the current of normal life' (DES A Language for Life, HMSO, 1975).

Yet almost everyone experiences poetry as a child, in the form of rhymes, games or chants. So what happens? How does poetry get lost along the path to adulthood? How does this 'language which consists of the best words in the best order, language used with the greatest possible inclusiveness and power' (ibid.) cease to have a place in people's lives?

Do you read poetry for pleasure? If not, is this because of the way you were taught? Did you relish Rossetti or worry about Wordsworth? Did you laugh with Lear or want to murder Milton? Did you have to persist with a poem like a dog with a bone or were you allowed to savour poetry, to roll the words around your mouth and fill your head with pictures and images?

Poets take ordinary things and, through their apposite and economic use of words, give them life and form for our pleasure and delight. They help us to discover new ways of looking at the world around us with fresh eyes and minds.

# BACKGROUND

Poetry is about imagination and imagery, seeing the normal with a perceptive eye, creating extraordinary visions from everyday things. Poetry for children should, above all else, give pleasure. It should open doors to the imagination, and at the same time be relevant and understandable to children. It should stimulate their thinking and give expression to their feelings, but, most importantly, it should be fun.

However, poetry is more than a quick laugh, and although poets like Michael Rosen and Spike Milligan are funny, they are more than that. Their comments are often shrewd, going deeper than the surface texture of the poem first suggests. Other poets like Kit Wright, Wes Magee, Moira Andrew, Judith Nicholls, Brian Patten and Roger McGough also often write with wry humour as well as with serious intentions, and both moods can be equally appealing to children.

Poetry has to be both caught and taught. Children need to be doused in it, drowned in it, immersed in it, surrounded by it, so that they feel that it is part of their everyday life.

## What is poetry?

Poetry is an art form which opens the windows of the imagination. It can often seem immediately relevant in a unique way. It leads to thought and reflection and it develops, categorises and extends vocabulary. It is not simply a flush of florid phrases, which may detract from the image. Adjectives have to work for their living!

Poetry can call up a remembered moment, feeling or experience. A poem can often suggest links with our own experiences, and enable us to see them in a different light.

Poetry is a way of extending our knowledge, of making us aware of important issues, as well as providing a means of escape and a source of humour in life's circumstances. It can also present us with the dark, grim side of life.

Poetry can be fiction, fantasy or very real. It can comment on our immediate world, conjure the future or hold us in the grip of the past. Poetry can be lyrical or terse, a conversation or a ballad, a nursery rhyme or a playground chant, a song or a play on words.

Good poetry is rather like an onion, where the peeling back of each layer reveals a finer one beneath. An impression is gained from the first superficial reading of a poem, but successive readings may reveal meanings previously hidden.

Charles Causley, in *The Puffin Book of Magic Verse* writes that: 'A poem is more than a mere arrangement of words on paper, or on the tongue. Its hints, suggestions, the echoes it sets off in the mind, and its omissions... all join up with the reader's thoughts and feelings and make a kind of magical union'.

A poet uses imagery and allusion, sound and shape as much as a precise choice of words and phrases to draw in the reader. But often most important of all is the effect that poetry has when it is read aloud. It is by the spoken word, its rhythm, cadence, fluidity, suggestion, hint or incantation, that we are drawn in.

## Why teach poetry?

Encounters with poetry help us to reflect upon and shape our experiences. Through poetry, we can come to know ourselves and our world differently; we can hear something essential to ourselves, something we recognise instinctively as a truth.

Words are the tools we use to externalise experience. Ted Hughes, in *Poetry in the Making (Faber and Faber)*, writes that through poetry: '...it is occasionally possible, just for brief moments, to find words that will unlock the doors of all those many mansions inside the head and express something... of the deep complexity that makes us precisely the way we are.'

Through poetry a child's imagination is opened to many opportunities for his own writing. He learns to use words more exactly, mastering them and making them work for him. Encountering poems can be a far better way of learning to read than weeks of work on reading skills and comprehension exercises. It is a language lesson that reveals how language can both empower and enslave. As a means of self-expression for a child, it is immeasurably valuable.

Poetry fosters language and learning. It deepens children's skills in language and extends them through interesting and pleasurable activities.

## Writing poetry

When we introduce children to writing poetry we are not trying to create poets. What we want to do is to develop in them a keen sensitivity to imagery and feelings, and an awareness of the response of their senses. We want them to explore the nature and exact meaning of words, to be exposed to the rich language of poetry, to experience a diversity of texts, forms, styles and approaches and to assimilate them into their own writing.

It has often been said that children should be allowed to write freely and without interference or influence from the teacher, but just giving them a pencil and paper and expecting poetry to flow forth is like giving them a lump of clay and expecting them to fashion a beautiful pot. If they do not know how to work with clay their pots are likely to remain primitive in form and become misshapen or damaged in the firing. In the same way, without help, children are unlikely to develop the linguistic skills which will allow them to write freely and effectively.

Good writing takes time to develop, and it should not be left to chance. Like any other skill, it has to be taught in a developmental way. We have to take children from where they are, build on what they know and offer them a wide range of experiences from which they can grow.

They need to be able to write what they want to say freely, without inhibition. This is very much down to us, as teachers, and how we plan for and encourage our children's language to grow.

By judicious guidance and exposure to the styles of a wide range of authors, children can learn different techniques. By plundering a

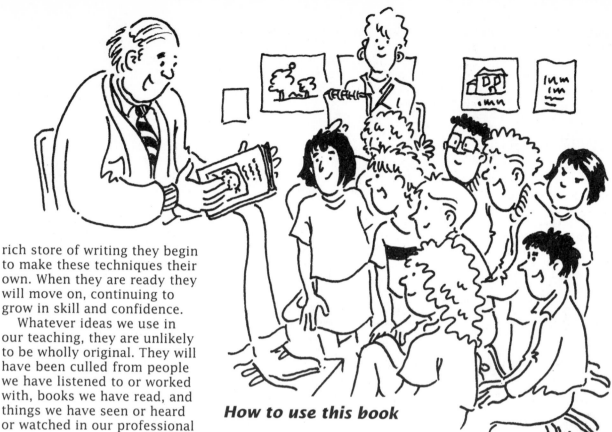

rich store of writing they begin to make these techniques their own. When they are ready they will move on, continuing to grow in skill and confidence.

Whatever ideas we use in our teaching, they are unlikely to be wholly original. They will have been culled from people we have listened to or worked with, books we have read, and things we have seen or heard or watched in our professional life. What makes an idea our own is how we adapt it and make it work for us and our pupils.

The influences at work within this book are gathered from a number of sources: from a course led by Moira Andrew and Wes Magee who gave me so many ideas for working with poetry in schools; from watching Judith Nicholls draw poetry from even the youngest infants; from studying with Michael Benton; from Pie Corbett, Sandy Brownjohn, Ted Hughes and Mike Rosen; and from reading and sharing poetry with the children from five to twelve with whom I have worked over the years. The pleasure we have had from sharing poetry and the thrill and excitement of writing our own have formed these inspirations for poetry.

## How to use this book

This book is designed to help children to listen, speak, read, write, think about and enjoy poetry. Because of the nature of the activities, they will also lift the quality of all children's language work. The book contains practical ideas which have been developed in the classroom, suggestions for using poetry across the curriculum and ways of presenting poetry. Photocopiable material is also provided to support the text where appropriate.

Each chapter is divided into three sections: the introduction highlights the important aspects needing consideration; the background discusses specific issues relevant to the chapter; and the activities section provides practical ideas for stimulating children's work on poetry, covering both content and process. All the tasks have been designed to have meaning and purpose for the child.

Each activity indicates the optimum number of children who can work together on each task, and the age range for which the activity is intended. These are intended to be guidelines only; much is dependent on what the children themselves bring to poetry and their previous experience of writing and listening. Therefore, you should choose widely from these activities to suit the needs of your children and your planned programme of work.

## Overview

The overall pattern of this book is that each chapter builds on the previous one or sets the scene for those to come.

First, we look at beginning to enjoy poetry for its own sake, learning some poems and taking ownership of them. Then we turn to look at writing poetry together, getting started and the processes involved. These processes apply to poetry in particular, but also to all writing in general. From process we turn to tools of different kinds; words, knowledge about language and the use of different poetic forms. Next, we look at broadening poetry across the curriculum, using it for specific purposes. Finally, support materials are provided in the form of photocopiable material and resources.

### Poetry with beginners

In some ways beginning poetry is easy because it has the freedom of early writing, before the agonies of how to write and spell overtake the writer, but it is also difficult because of the problem of knowing where and how to start.

This first chapter looks at reading poetry, including simple ways of exploring its content, and provides suggestions for beginning to write poetry, working from the known and familiar.

### Oral and traditional poetry

We want children to develop a love of poetry, to enjoy reading it, to dip willingly into its treasure house of language and ideas. We want them to be excited by it, to want to share it with others, to say 'Listen to this one, I think it's great!'.

We also want them to build up their own store of oral poetry and to become familiar with the traditional chants and rhymes that are part of our literary and cultural heritage.

We want them to be able to talk about the ideas, experiences and emotions a poem contains, to go beneath the surface meaning of a poem or rhyme and to investigate its deeper meaning.

In Chapter 2 various ways are suggested of helping children to talk about poetry and to build on their own collection of words, chants and rhymes.

### Ways of getting started

How do we get children started along the poetry-writing path? What means can be adopted to get them going? In Chapter 3 we look at ways of getting children started. Ways are suggested of making use of their thoughts, of bringing relevant words to the forefront of their minds and of putting words down on paper.

Suggestions are also made for using a wealth of stimuli and experiences to initiate poetry writing.

### Processes

Chapter 4 looks at the processes involved in actually writing poetry, from the kernel of an idea right through to publication.

It suggests ways of working on a poem and honing it, using redrafting, revising and editing techniques. Surface errors, both secretarial and technical, are discussed as well as ways of presenting the final copy.

### Word play

Words are the tools that we use to give voice to our thoughts, ideas, concerns and emotions. Chapter 5 looks at a range of word games and techniques designed to stimulate vocabulary development. The emphasis of this chapter is on playing with words to release tensions and anxieties and to overcome the common fear of 'getting it wrong'.

### Making words work and choosing words

The activities in Chapter 6 are a continuation of the fun and games of the previous chapter. Children are encouraged to search out a range of similar words, to explore their exact meaning and to select the most apposite one.

Children are helped to use a thesaurus and to locate words speedily in any word-finder.

### Knowledge about language

Frequently, adults avoid using certain words or terms because they are thought to be conceptually too difficult for children to comprehend. Why is one word more difficult than the next? Why avoid words like hexagon or parallelogram, noun or verb, alliteration or synonym? Children love to investigate them, to roll them round their tongues and show them off when an opportunity presents itself.

Chapter 7 provides a number of practical ideas and suggestions for helping children to develop their knowledge about language.

### All kinds of poetry

The children should now be ready to look at particular types of poetry. A wide range is offered in Chapter 8, and more can be found in the books which are suggested in the bibliography. This chapter looks at some of the poetic forms most suited to primary school children and suggests a series of tasks to help children write within a given framework.

We are often told that small is beautiful, and so it is, but if poetry is to make an impact, it has to be perfectly formed. Chapter 8 suggests ways of achieving this.

### Poetry across the curriculum

Chapter 9 looks at ways of working with poetry across a range of subject areas. The activities suggest ways of applying poetry to various themes, including aspects of science, history, geography, personal and social education, art and media studies.

### Parading poetry

Poetry needs an audience. Sometimes we are our own audience; for example, when compiling a personal anthology, but during poetry weeks and presentations the audience can be the whole school. Poetry needs to come out of its élitist closet, to be visible. Chapter 10 suggests ways of making this happen.

### Resources and bibliography

Look at the poetry books on offer in your classroom. When did you last add to them? A wider selection of collections and anthologies is available than ever before.

The choice of suitable material is a matter of personal taste, yours and the children's. Chapter 11 lists a number of published anthologies, collections and 'how to' books as well as posters, photographs and useful addresses to support teaching poetry.

### Photocopiable pages

This section includes pages to support work on particular activities mentioned in the book, as well as photocopiable frames and borders that can be used to help children with the presentation of their poems, and word resources to inspire their writing.

## Conclusion

This book is not intended to be a complete guide to teaching poetry. It simply suggests different ways of providing opportunities for children to encounter poetry and to experience it through a range of approaches and activities. It is meant to guide you through what can be a difficult subject (and one which is often avoided) and to give you all kinds of 'inspirations for poetry'!

# CHAPTER 1

# Poetry with beginners

'Poetry begins in delight.... With young children, above all, our rightful concern is with this delight', writes Mike Benton ('Poetry for Children: A Neglected Art', Children's Literature in Education, 9 [3]). Many children will have already found this delight early on in their childhood, while others will have been less fortunate.

Children enter school with a varied amount of acquired knowledge across a widely differing range of experiences and varying levels of competence in linguistic skills. In five short years they have learned to communicate in words. They have developed, in varying degrees, a breadth of vocabulary and the ability to say words in sequential order, making utterances that can be understood. With increasing skill, over the years, they have learned to make language work for them.

# BACKGROUND

Babies first demand by crying, then they learn to manipulate others to get what they want. Gradually, young children become skilful at coercion and learn to request, inform, describe and explain to make their needs and ideas understood. Even the youngest children will enjoy experiencing and experimenting with new words, rhymes and rhythms.

We are, therefore, not so much teaching poetry from scratch, as building on a formidable array of learned linguistic skills.

Children do not come to school as blank books waiting to be written on. They will all have something written on most pages – it is just the amount that varies. We have to find out how much they already know in order to plan their future learning.

This chapter looks at beginnings – beginning to move on from nursery rhymes, beginning to explore poems and beginning to write poetry.

## Getting hooked on poetry

How do children get hooked on poetry, and how can we use the linguistic skills that children bring to school to attract them to poetry?

First of all, give poetry a prominent place in your daily plan. Introduce poems and rhymes when the children are gathered around you for a story or a talk session. Say or read every poem at least twice at any one session, more if the children are willing.

Children need time to absorb and reflect on what they hear and read, and to consider their feelings and responses. Often we jump in too quickly to find out what they think. After a first reading, wait a few moments, then read the poem again before you begin to talk about it with them. They may not always understand all the words or phrases in a poem, or its context, but the language is often such that they will be swept along by it. If you establish this way of listening to poetry, children very quickly respond.

Put up posters and pictures which contain short verses or rhyming couplets, and read the rhymes to, and then with, the children. Display a book open at a different poem every day, together with a label saying 'Today's poem'. Develop the label over time, for example, 'What did you think of today's poem?', 'When you read today's poem I want you to think about...' and so on.

Many early picture books use well-known poems and rhymes. Use them. Put them in your poetry corner. These books will soon be known by heart and will help support any learning-to-read programme.

## Beginning writing poetry

In the early years children often speak for the pleasure of speaking rather than to communicate. This early speech can be likened to poetry in that its concern is to celebrate and mourn, not to instruct and inform. It is this personal speech that we try to capture when we first lead children along the path to writing poetry. You should try to use their own words as much as possible to create poems together, choosing subjects that are familiar to them, such as parts of the body, family, friends, home, toys and so on. Tell the children about your memories from your own childhood and let them talk about things that have happened to them that they remember clearly.

Children see things from a different point of view from adults. Use their perspective when writing group poems. Irrespective of attainment, all children can take part in making rhymes. Introduce redrafting from the start, so that it becomes an accepted part of writing. Help children to look for words that can be left out or that are ambiguous.

Poetry brings in all the language modes, and it forms an essential part of speaking and listening, reading and writing, presentation and performance. But most of all our concern must be to foster children's delight in sharing and making poetry.

# ...What do they know?

## Age range
Five to six.

## Group size
The whole class.

## What you need
A flipchart or large sheet of paper, a thick felt-tipped pen.

## What to do
Many children will have learned rhymes and songs before coming into school, so take advantage of what they already know. Sit with them in your carpeted area and sing or say a familiar nursery rhyme. Write the heading 'Rhymes we know' on the piece of paper and then write the title of the one you have just sung to begin the list. Ask the children to suggest another rhyme, sing it together and then write it down.

Number the rhymes as you write them on the list, and pin the list up in the classroom where the children can read it.

Let the children who are willing, perform a rhyme or song on their own and then ask the others to join in the second time around. Always add the rhymes they know to the list.

The list has a two-fold advantage. First, it is a record of what the children know, and it is important for the children to realise what they know. Many of them will be surprised at the way the list grows. Second, in rhyme-time, children who go to the list to choose a rhyme for the class to say can read the number and the title. At different times during the day you will see huddles of children around the list reading it and discussing it.

The rhymes on your list become the common ground your pupils share, on which you can base your curriculum planning for poetry.

# 2. Make it up

## Age range
Five to six.

## Group size
The whole class.

## What you need
No special requirements.

## What to do
Instead of telling the children what to do when they are about to begin a new activity, try singing your instructions to a familiar tune. In no time at all the children will join in with you, and they will do as you ask with good humour! For example, using the tune 'Here we go round the mulberry bush', you could sing 'Let's get ready for PE', or, 'Now's the time to clear away/change your shoes/come for a story...'; whatever is appropriate.

## Further activity
Divide the class into groups of four to make up an 'instruction' rhyme. When they have completed it, each group can sing their instruction rhyme to the rest of the class. You can then use the children's rhymes at suitable times.

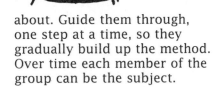

# 3. All about me

### Age range
Five to six.

### Group size
The whole class and groups of four.

### What you need
A flipchart or large sheet of paper, a felt-tipped pen.

### What to do
Ask the children to tell you what they see when they look at you and write their statements on the chart, one beneath the other.

Ask the children to look at the lengths of each line. Is each line the same length or are they all different? Tap out the syllables of each line and ask the children to join in with you. Write the number of taps for each line at the end of the line. Could any words be cut out or could the lines be said a different way so that the number of taps is the same for each line? Rewrite the new versions of the lines.

You can now look at the order of the lines. Are they in the best order? The children should reorder the lines until they are happy with the finished result. You can then write up the final version in your best writing on photocopiable page 180.

### Further activity
Divide the children into groups of four and ask them to choose one child in the group to write about. Guide them through, one step at a time, so they gradually build up the method. Over time each member of the group can be the subject.

# 4. Who's this?

### Age range
Five to seven.

### Group size
The whole class and groups of four.

### What you need
A flipchart or large sheet of paper, a felt-tipped pen.

### What to do
Describe one of the children in the class. Without looking at the child say four things about her, for example, short fair hair, pale blue eyes, red jumper, long trousers. Ask the children who they think this is. Repeat the description and tap the syllables of each word as you say it. Invite the children to join in. Ask for a volunteer and tell the other children to describe him as you did. Write up the phrases on the flipchart and look at ways of organising them to create a poem.

After older children have worked through two or three examples, divide them into groups and ask them to work out a description of someone in another group. They should try to make each line three syllables long. They can then either choose one child in the group to say their 'poem' or each child can say a line of the description and say the last line, when they ask 'Who is it?', all together.

They can also write poems with two-, three- or four-beat lines, and lengthen or change the last line if they so choose. The 'poem' can then be read out to the class and displayed.

# 5. Brothers and sisters

### Age range
Five to seven.

### Group size
The whole class or small groups.

### What you need
Paper, pencils, *Midnight Forest* by Judith Nicholls (Faber and Faber).

## 6. Familiar things

### Age range
Five to seven.

### Group size
The whole class or small groups.

### What you need
A flipchart or large sheets of paper, a thick felt-tipped pen, a familiar object.

### What to do
It is important that children learn to create images with words and develop their language. In this activity, therefore, you record the children's thoughts which they can then express without worrying about writing or spelling.

Choose a familiar object together. It could be something:
• brought back from a walk or a visit;
• brought into the class for a show and tell session;
• found by a child and brought to school;
• from a topic table.

The list is endless, but it must be possible to put the object in front of the children as they work. Ask them questions about the object:
• Where did it come from?
• What is it like?

says that makes them cross, or use the pattern of Judith Nicholls' poem:

Tell me a story!
Lend me that book!...

### Further activities
• Read 'Your brother Danny' by Michael Rosen in *You Can't Catch Me (Puffin)*. Talk about the poem, mentioning the nonsense element, and ask the children to write one themselves, but beginning 'My brother/sister's got...'.
• Read 'Last into bed' by Michael Rosen in *You Can't Catch Me*. Are the children teased and/or scared sometimes by a brother or sister? Do older siblings get a bit bossy, as in 'I'm the Youngest in our House' in *You Can't Catch Me*? How do their parents react? How do the children themselves handle it? Talk about the best way to cope with teasing inside as well as outside the family.

### What to do
Read together Judith Nicholls' poem 'Sister...' from *Midnight Forest*. Ask the children questions about themselves, for example: 'How old are you? Do you have a brother or a sister? Do they make you cross? What sort of things do they do?'

Relate any incidents from your childhood concerning brothers or sisters.

Return to the subject of the children's families. Put up a list of words the children suggest to you about the things that make them cross.

One starter line for a poem could be, for example, 'I get cross when...', or start with something the brother or sister

• What do we know about it?
• How did we find out these things? (The children are likely to suggest that they found them out by looking at the object.)

Draw round your right hand, palm down, (or left hand, palm up) on a flipchart or large sheet of paper. On the thumb write the word 'see'. Then write 'hear', 'touch', 'taste', and 'smell', going from left to right, on the rest of the fingers. Above the thumb record the words the children use to describe what the object looks like. Make the list quickly; it does not need to be long, and four or five words will suffice.

Cover or hide the object and go over the list with the children. Ask them if the words that you have written down give a clear picture of what the object looks like. Put a line through any words that they reject.

Show the children the item again. Does it make a sound? Can we hear anything if we shake it? You can then make another list, above the first finger, of words to describe what the object sounds like. Continue making lists for the rest of the senses in the same manner.

Go through the lists again, looking for words to reject. By doing this the children are beginning to learn to edit, a skill they will need to employ to greater effect as they go through primary school.

Create a simple poem together from their ideas. For example, suppose an attractive leaf is the object. The children might say that it is green, pointed and thin; it flies and

flutters; it crackles and sounds like paper; it feels light, smooth, prickly and dry; it smells sharp and earthy and makes them think of Christmas. The poem may be something like this:

> The leaf is green and
>    and pointed and thin
> It crackles when I press it,
> It feels light and smooth and
>    prickly,
> It smells sharp and earthy,
> Holly makes me think of
>    Christmas.

Let the children watch you as you redraft the poem and write it out in 'best'. Tell them why you are doing this. Finally, read it to them and display it for them to read.

### Further activity
Ask the children for any images that the object may suggest, and then develop another poem with them.

# 7. What are we made of?

### Age range
Five to eight.

### Group size
The whole class or groups of four.

### What you need
A flipchart or large sheets of paper, a thick felt-tipped pen.

### What to do

Say the nursery rhyme 'What are little boys made of?' twice, and then ask the children to join in with you. Talk about the rhyme. Are boys really like that? Could the children remake the rhyme to show what little boys are really like?

Write the children's suggestions on the large sheets of paper. Work on them with the children by asking questions so that the statements fit the rhyme. On a fresh piece of paper, write the new verse and put it up beside the draft that you have worked on together.

Repeat this process for the verse about girls. Although the youngest children may need a break before going on to do this, older children may be able to work on the second verse in groups. They can then all look together at the variations which each group has come up with. Display the different verses side by side.

Use this opportunity to talk with the children about stereotyping and remind them to look for it in books they read, in the media and at home.

### Further activities

• Older children can rewrite the rhyme from different viewpoints, for example, that of a parent or a teacher.
• Ask the children to find out and write about what we are really made of. Could a poem be made about that?

# 8. Hands on

### Age range
Five to nine.

### Group size
The whole class and pairs.

### What you need
*You Can't Catch Me* by Michael Rosen (Puffin), paper, pencils, felt-tipped pens.

### What to do
Read to the children 'This is the hand' by Michael Rosen in *You Can't Catch Me*. Ask them to examine their own hands. What are they like? Tell them to draw round one of their hands carefully, copying the shape and pattern of the nails, the lines and wrinkles. Older children can then write in the hand its predominant physical attributes; the texture of the skin, the number of bones they can feel in the fingers and the palm, the joints and the ways in which the hand and the fingers move.

With younger children talk about hands, what they can do and explore their attributes, movement and control. Once the children have done this,

ask them to draw around their hands again and this time write in the different things hands can do.

Let the children compare their hands with a partner's. To what extent are they the same and to what extent are they different? Ask them to think what they do with their hands when they are calm, cross, caring, hurt or carrying something.

Read the poem again to the children. What did Michael Rosen say his hands could do?

Ask them to write three lines starting each line with 'My hands can...'. The fourth line should say 'I'm glad I've got hands'.

Some children will be able to write more than one verse. Older children might like to copy the poem's format; for example, 'This is the hand that...', or write metaphors ('My hands are...') and similes ('My hands are like...').

Display the poems with cut-outs or pictures of the children's hands around them. You could also display examples of things hands wear, use and make.

## Further activities

• Ask the children to draw round each of their hands. They should write the good things a hand can do on one hand and the bad things on the other. They can use this information as the basis of another poem.

• Read together some other poems about hands; for example, the poems in *Sense and Nonsense – Touching* compiled by Susanne and Shona McKellar (Macdonald); 'Hands are cold' from *Dragon's Smoke*, collected by Wes Magee (Basil Blackwell); 'Hands' by Brian Levison and 'Hands' by Peter Young, both in *My Red Poetry Book* edited by Moira Andrew (Macmillan).

• Ask the children to take off their shoes and socks and examine their feet. Adapt the ideas given for work on hands to feet.

• Read poems about feet, for example 'Footprints' by John Travers Moore in *Another First Poetry Book* compiled by John Foster (Oxford University Press); 'If you don't put your shoes on' by Michael Rosen in *You Can't Catch Me* (Puffin); 'Old man of Peru', Anon, in *Shadow Dance*, collected by Adrian Rumble (Cassell); and 'The feet' by Tom Wayman in *A World of Poetry* selected by Michael Rosen (Kingfisher).

# 9. Working with poems

## Age range
Five to eleven.

## Group size
The whole class and small groups.

## What you need
A suitable poem, a cassette and cassette player, paper, felt-tipped pens, plastic folders, a hole punch, a ring file.

## What to do
Before you begin this activity familiarise yourself with a poem. Read it to yourself several times and try reading it

out aloud in different ways until you have caught the feel of it.

Once you know the poem really well you can then read or say it to the class. Read it to them several times. Warn the children that often the first time someone hears a poem it can seem difficult to understand, but if they concentrate while they are listening they will soon come to know what it is about. Even so, don't choose poems that cause them to reach too far, as you could put them off poetry altogether.

Make sure that the children have understood any words that could be beyond their experience (you may discover that they know more than you think), but do not discuss them at this stage.

Draw parallels with your own and their experiences and talk about them. Compare their thoughts on the poem and encourage them to see that people can take different messages from the same poem.

Record the poem twice on tape and play the tape to the class the next day. Encourage the children to join in with the second reading.

Ask them what they think the poem is about. What conclusions can they draw from it?

If the poem is about a person or animal, you could role-play the part of the character and let the children ask you questions to help their understanding.

Discuss the role-playing with the children. Has it helped them to understand the character or filled in the background for them?

Read the poem or say it together over the next few days at odd moments. Mount a copy of the poem on card and cover it with self-adhesive plastic. Ask the children to put their names on a list if they would like to take the poem home to read to their family. Later, place the poem in a plastic wallet or punch holes in it and put it in a class anthology (see page 169). Leave the anthology in the book corner for the children to read. They will be surprised at the way the collection grows.

### Further activity
Supply a list of 'character' poems for children to select from. They can work together in small groups, with one of them role-playing the character. This pupil needs to have access to the poem over a couple of days to get under the skin of the character, so that he or she can respond to questions from the group about the character and his or her reactions in the poem.

# 10. Anthology tapes

### Age range
Five to eleven.

### Group size
The whole class or small groups.

### What you need
Video or audio cassettes and players, a range of suitable poems, paper and pens, volunteers to read poems.

### What to do
Make up tapes with groups of five poems on them. The poems can have a common theme, or they can just be favourites. Record each one twice, the first time just for listening, and the second for joining in. Ask friends (especially people whom the children do not know) to record the poems on the cassette or video-tape. Try to have some readers of the opposite sex from you. Children's attention is caught by different voices, and it also gives them a rest from yours! The range of voices draws attention to the universal appeal of poetry, and shows that it is not just something we 'do' in school. Make two or three copies of the poems read, and place them with the cassettes so the children can follow the words while listening.

# 11. Exploring the content

### Age range
Five to eleven.

### Group size
The whole class or small groups.

### What you need
Pictures and photographs, cutting and mounting materials, paper and pens, poetry anthologies, materials for children's art work, audio cassettes and recorder.

### What to do
The following are suggestions for working with poems. Select from them and use those best suited to the chosen poem.
• Introduce a poem to the children. Talk about it with them. What pictures does it conjure up in their minds? What does it make them think about?
• Set up a display of pictures and photographs related to a poem or theme you are working on, and taken from magazines found by you and the children. These help children to regard the theme in different lights and stimulate their language production.

• Make an anthology of poems that echo the same theme. The anthology can be illustrated with the children's drawings. Young children will be able to suggest some from their known repertoire of rhymes and poems, and together you can explore available books for other suitable additions. The more children work with poetry, and the more their reading improves, the more readily they will find poems for the anthologies.
• The children can draw or paint pictures and make collages to show their thoughts and ideas about a particular poem. Display their artwork with a copy of the poem.
• Record a poem or song a number of times for the children to listen to as they paint. For older children use a 'mood' group of poems or songs.
• Some children can mime to a poem while others recite it. They should say it in a dramatic or funny way or tell it as an anecdote or story. Make a play out of the poem using the same words but expanding it from its original condensed form.

# 12. A rhyme a day

### Age range
Five to eleven.

### Group size
The whole class.

### What you need
A selection of poetry books and stories which contain repetitions or choruses.

### What to do
Read a new rhyme to the children every day. Use any spare moments to go through new ones. Children will quickly learn new rhymes and they will soon become a part of a child's repertoire.

A good way to help the children learn these rhymes is, as soon as you think they are ready, to begin to leave out a rhyming word, the end of a line, the last line or the chorus when you read out the poem. The children will quickly start to respond and soon they will be joining in with the whole rhyme.

Don't forget to add new rhymes to your list!

### Further activity
Do the same with repeated lines or choruses in stories such as 'Run, run, as fast as you can, you can't catch me, I'm the...', or 'Mirror, mirror on the wall, who is the fairest...'. As the phrases are repeated several times, the children will be able to join in before the end of the story, even when hearing the story for the first time.

# CHAPTER 2

# Oral and traditional poetry

Poetry has survived orally for centuries. The vast majority of the population used to be unable to read, and they felt that this lyrical language passed down their history and protected them from evil. Wandering minstrels and story-tellers were most people's only way of knowing what was happening in the world beyond their village.

Today, both past and present events are written down, but many stories and poems are still transmitted by word of mouth. Parents repeat to their toddlers the rhymes, chants, lullabies, finger rhymes, singing games and action rhymes of their own childhood, so preparing children for the wealth of poetry yet to come.

Poetry is rich, full and varied. There is something in it for everyone. Reading poetry not only gives pleasure and enjoyment, it also plays an important part in developing the appreciation of images and sound, rhyme and rhythm, pattern and form.

# BACKGROUND

## Listening to poetry

Coleridge writes about 'that willing suspension of disbelief for the moment which constitutes poetic faith' (*Biographia Literaria,* Chapter 14, 1817). Children can do this more readily than adults. James Britton agrees, believing that the period up to the age of eleven is the 'golden age' for listening to poetry ('The Role of Fantasy' in *English in Education* No.5, 1971) . Children, during these early years, are much more responsive to poetry than many teachers give them credit for, whereas the teachers, as adults, are more distanced from its appeal.

Poetry needs to be listened to, but children are seldom given enough opportunities to listen. If they are surrounded with poetry children's abilities to listen, read and concentrate are developed automatically, and they are also helped to listen creatively. They learn to build pictures in their minds from the words, images and sounds and, in turn, to use imagery to explore their own ideas and feelings.

Children will be attracted to poetry by your enthusiasm and by the ability you have to make a poem come alive for them. If you want them to enjoy poetry you, the reader, need to be able to bring out the qualities of the poem.

Sometimes children may not understand a word of a poem but will listen spellbound to the lilt of the language, the nuances of sound, the evocative nature of the words or the glimmer of what is lurking underneath the surface. Even the nonsense lines in rhymes, like 'Whipsee diddle dee dandy dee', or 'Wisky, wasky, weedle', have a magic for small children.

There is so much poetry to draw upon that there is something for every pupil, whatever their age or ability. Poetry anthologies provide a rich resource, but in order to listen to a poem, you have to say it out loud, to hear it outside your head. Only then will you know whether it is one you can use to build up your own storehouse of oral and traditional poetry for your children to listen to.

## Sharing poetry

Choosing poems to share with your class means that you yourself must read and reread poetry. It is important that you read to the children poetry that *you* enjoy. Share with them the reasons why you like it and what it is about the poem that appeals to you, so that they know the pleasure it gives you. It is your enthusiasm that will make poetry come alive for children and 'sell' it to them.

Sometimes you will find an adult poem that you think the children might like. There is only one way to find out, and that is to read it to them! One year's group may delight in it, the next may be left cold, but isn't it the same with adults too?

Read lots of poetry aloud to the whole class. Try to find time for at least one poem a day, but preferably more. This way you will help to foster a love of poetry. When reading to the children you must know the poem well so that you can read it fluently. Reading a poem is a presentation, not something to be stumbled over with your nose buried in the book. What impression are we giving to children of the value of poetry if we ourselves do not give it status? Let poetry become part of the day, something worth giving time to and something very real and important to share.

When children are sharing poems they need to know that reading a poem aloud for the first time can be difficult and that sharing is a performance, however small the audience. They need to know that you can't just take a book off the shelf, pick out a poem and read it out in such a way as to give an impression of its qualities and meaning. A poem has to be practised out loud several times in order for the reader to become sensitive to the nuances of its language, to feel the rhythm, to sense the meaning and be able to convey it to the listener.

## Learning poetry

Poetry learned in childhood remains with us, for us to share and to pass on to the next generation. The sheer love of words is something we need to keep hold of and help children to develop throughout their school years.

Learning poetry needs to be encouraged and developed. It does not happen by itself. We should carry on building on the foundations laid by the child's family, when language was heard but not yet spoken.

Don't ignore Anglo-Saxon, Medieval and Elizabethan poetry. Older poetry is often highly accessible to primary children; it was written to be delivered orally to an illiterate audience and so is real and concrete, not a minefield of intellectual and linguistic complexity.

Children are able to savour and enjoy ballads, laments, work songs, folk songs and sea shanties. So sing folk songs like 'The wraggle taggle gypsies', laments like 'The water is wide', ballads like 'Barbara Allen', 'The trees they do grow high' or 'Stewball'; and lullabies like 'Hush little baby', especially if you play an instrument.

Narrative poems with their vivid descriptions, repetition, alliteration and themes of loyalty and courage, appeal to children's sense of ritual and have considerable influence on their knowledge and use of language. *Beowulf, The Canterbury Tales, Sir Gawain and the Green Knight* all fall into this category. At nine I learned *The Pied Piper of Hamelin* (Robert Browning) and still find a special magic in reciting: 'Hamelin Town's in Brunswick, By famous Hanover city...'. The verse 'Rats' stands by itself and is successful with children as young as seven. By nine, they are ready for the spell cast by Shakespeare's three witches from *Macbeth* (IV.i), beginning, 'Round about the cauldron go...' and finishing '...like a hell-broth boil and bubble'.

Poetry, once learned, becomes part of us for the rest of our lives, whether it is couplets, stanzas, lines or whole poems. Poems remembered from childhood may range from Christina Rossetti's delightful 'Mix a pancake', or her moving 'In the bleak mid-winter', via the humour of Lewis Carroll's 'The time has come, the Walrus said' or 'You are old, Father William...', to Jaques' speech from Shakespeare's *As You Like It* ( II.v).

## Rhyme and rhythm

Rhyme and rhythm are just as much a part of a young child's life as story, with songs and nursery rhymes, rhythmic games and movement and counting rhymes. As they progress through the primary years the power of rhythm and rhyme often lessens. The chants and rhymes of playground games are updated to make them relevant to the children's lives for a little longer, but the power and magic of poetry has gone for many children. We need to look at how we can keep it alive as children grow to adulthood.

Traditional poems are powerful aids to reading because they have meaning, they contain stories concisely and economically told, they are often humorous, and they can be learned quickly and shared.

Peter Bryant and Lynette Bradley's research (*Children's Reading Problems,* Blackwell, 1985) shows that pre-school experience of nursery rhymes enables children to recognise phonological patterns such as alliteration and rhyme, and plays a critical role in determining early reading success. Children who have not developed this phonological awareness at school entry are likely to have difficulties in learning to read and developing reading fluency.

Nursery rhymes are a must for all sorts of reasons, not least because they are part of our heritage and our history. Look how concise, appropriate and accurate 'Ring-a-ring of roses' is when studying the Great Plague of 1665!

I believe that both rhythm and rhyme are essential in the first poetry that children hear, but by the time they reach early juniors rhyme should form only part of their diet, although rhythm remains essential.

Young children chant, intone, sing, speak and sound new words, alliterative phrases, nursery rhymes, number rhymes, street rhymes, game rhymes, not just because of their strong simple rhythms and powerful rhymes, but also because of the sound of the words themselves. We must try not to destroy this sheer love of oral language.

## Working on a poem

If a poem is well received by your class there are two avenues which can be pursued.

First, you can simply enjoy rereading the poem and learning it. Even the simplest poetry cannot be taken in at one hearing, it must be heard again and again until it sits comfortably in the head. For primary children it is the listening, feeling, thinking and reading that is important. Sometimes you need to say nothing, just allow the poem to sink in.

Rereading the poem tells you how well it is being received by the children. If it is not going down well and it doesn't arouse enthusiasm, move on to another poem, or another activity. There may come a time, later in the year, when you can try out the poem again. You can say 'Do you remember that poem we read on...' and read it again. This time it could be the right moment to share the poem. Sometimes a different

approach will work, but if you feel it has died a death – leave it alone. It may not work with this year's class but could set next year's alight.

Second, you can work on the poem. It may take several readings before the right time comes to talk about it in detail. Not all poetry is easily understood and your knowledge of the children will tell you when, or if, to lead them on to consider and reflect upon a poem's meaning.

By concentrating first on one part of the poem, then on another, following separate threads until the children gain a concept of the poem as a whole, you can begin to bring out its qualities. The length of time and the depth you give to this study depends upon the children's age, experience and the appropriateness of the poem.

If it is appropriate, some of the qualities you may want to explore could include:
• mood – humour, pathos, joy, haunting quality, other-worldliness;
• the effect of words and sound patterns;

• the images the poem creates;
• its care, concern, humanity;
• the shape it creates on the page and the effect this has upon the reader.

Other ways of working on a poem include:
• making a dramatic reading using role-play;
• using it for creative art and craft work;
• mounting and displaying it;
• using it as a basis for a topic (see *Inspirations for English,* Scholastic Publications, pages 96 to 101);
• writing it up and putting it in the children's growing anthology.

Sometimes, just an informal chat is all that is needed. Don't ruin poetry for the children, as it may have been ruined for you, by too much questioning and in-depth study.

# ACTIVITIES

## 1. Put it up

### Age range
Five to six.

### Group size
The whole class.

### What you need
Large sheets of paper, a thick felt-tipped pen.

### What to do
Write up and display any new poem you introduce, and read it with the children. Children need to see the pattern a poem makes on the page. Many do not realise that it looks different from a story.

Early readers will be able to trace the displayed poem or rhyme with their fingers, reading it as they do so, becoming familiar with the words in it, words that they can then use in their writing.

### Further activity
Ask the children to find poems similar in topic, shape or pattern to those on display. Copy these poems and let them form part of the display.

## 2. Feel the rhythm

### Age range
Five to six.

### Group size
The whole class or smaller groups.

### What you need
A selection of untuned percussion instruments.

### What to do
Not all children can recognise or identify that poems and rhymes feel different from stories; that the words have a rhythm and the rhythm makes a pattern.

Start off with nursery rhymes that the children know well, like 'Twinkle, twinkle little star' and 'Baa, baa, black sheep', following with others such as 'London's burning', 'Lavender's blue', 'One, two, three, four, five', 'Five fat sausages' and 'Polly put the kettle on'.

Help the children to feel the rhythm of the words in these rhymes by tapping them. If you use two fingers tapped on the back of the hand, rather than clapping, you will have a quiet, controlled sound which you will be able to speak over.

Tap the rhythm of the words in the first line of a rhyme without actually saying the

play a line. Discuss with them which instruments would best represent the message the line carries.

## Further activity

Introduce the concept of a pulse or beat. Clap the strong beat of a rhyme and then write out the rhyme, underlining the strong beats like this:

> <u>Baa</u>, baa, <u>black</u> sheep,
> <u>Have</u> <u>you</u> any <u>wool</u>,
> <u>Yes</u> sir, <u>yes</u> sir,
> <u>Three</u> bags <u>full</u>.

Once the children can do this, divide the class into two groups, so that one group taps out the rhythm of the syllables and the other taps out the beat. Use wood blocks for the beat, or padded drum sticks on cymbals, rather than loud, clashing sounds. The children must be able to listen, and you need to keep your sanity when surrounded by sound.

words. Ask the children if it reminds them of a song they know. You may need to do this several times at first, but the children will soon catch on. Quite quickly they will offer to tap a line or even a whole rhyme for others to guess.

Once they can feel the rhythm, let them use untuned percussion instruments to tap out the rhythms. Use tambours or tambourines instead of drums and tap them with the tips of the fingers. Let groups of children take it in turns to

# 3. Say it in rhythm

## Age range
Five to six.

## Group size
The whole class.

## What you need
A tambour or a Chinese wood block.

## What to do
Give the children instructions through rhythm. Tap them out keeping strictly to the long and short beats of the words. Here are some ideas:
- — — — — (Please shut the door);
- – – – – (Put up your chairs);
- — — — — – – (Come to the mat and sit down).

Introduce these instructions one at a time when the children are sitting around you. Follow up by using them during that day. Slowly build up your repertoire. They are a boon and a blessing when you've lost your voice!

## Further activity
Divide the children into small groups and let them work out some instruction rhythms for themselves.

## 4. A ditty a day

### Age range
Five and upwards.

### Group size
The whole class.

### What you need
A selection of poems, a calendar with room to write on.

### What to do
Tell the children that they are going to take it in turns to read a poem every day. They can choose any poem they like from an anthology, or even one of their own poems. Put up a calendar so that they can sign up for their 'ditty day'. This way the children will be able to choose when to present their poem and they will know how much time they have to prepare for it.

Always have one or two poems on hand yourself or have children ready to be 'reserves' in case someone is absent – but don't let the absent one off the hook!

### Further activity
Older children can prepare a group poem to present to the class.

## 5. Preparing poems to share

### Age range
Five and upwards.

### Group size
The whole class.

### What you need
A suitable poem or rhyme which will divide into parts for different speakers, copies for the children, felt-tipped pens, highlighter pens.

### What to do
Devise a set of indicators to mark the poems you are preparing for your class to read. Begin with an easy rhyme and show the children how to use simple annotation to indicate whose turn it is to read what, for example:
- m = me;
- b = boys;
- g = girls;
- an initial letter to indicate a particular child (F = Farhana).

The children can also highlight their own lines to help them see more clearly when it is their turn to read.

You can introduce more advanced annotation for your own use, for example:
- underline letters, words or phrases to be emphasised;
- use the music marks *pp*, *p*, *f*, *ff* to indicate the strength of voice needed for different lines, from whispering softness to very loud;
- put an arrow at the end of a line to indicate that one line carries over to the next without a pause, for example:

> There's none so rare as can compare→
> With King Cole and his fiddlers three';

• use an upward-sloping line to indicate a lifting voice and a downward slant for the opposite;
• break lines to emphasise a slight pause, for example:

/ And with it
\     a thimble, too!

• Use initial letters to indicate the different characters in a poem. Use 'N' for the narrator, for example:

**N** *f*    Ten little mice sat down to spin,
   *p*    Pussy came by and popped her head in.
**P** *f/*    'What you are *doing* my little men?'
**M** *p\*    'We're making coats for gentlemen.'
**P** *f/*    'Shall I come in and *bite* off your threads?'
**M** *f\*    'Oh no Mistress Pussy, you'll *bite* off our *heads*.'

Older pupils can learn to use all these marks themselves for their poetry reading or choral speaking.

# 6. Choral speaking

### Age range
Five and upwards.

### Group size
The whole class or groups of up to eight.

### What you need
Suitable poems, felt-tipped pens, highlighter pens.

### What to do
The way a poem is divided for choral speaking must depend on the dictates of the poem, not on how many children are in a class or group. Those not taking part should become the audience. The audience plays an important role, so let the listeners feel that their role matters to the whole performance. See that the shy child performs and the confident child is part of the audience so that the roles are kept in balance.

Read the poem several times to the children. As they become familiar with it, they will join in.

'Froggie went a-courting' lends itself to group narration with solo speakers for Mr Frog, Mistress Mouse and Uncle Rat.

Sometimes solo lines can be spoken by groups, for example: 'Where are you going to my pretty maid?' could be said by one group of children facing another group who will say the response. Similarly, 'Soldier, soldier, won't you marry me...' can be performed by two solo speakers and a narrative group, or by three groups.

Give older children copies of the poem that they are going to perform so that they can highlight the lines they are to read on their copies. They can also write instructions for reading and make other notes about speed and rhythm with felt-tipped pens. These copies can go into their collection to be prepared for their anthology at another time.

Encourage children to make the reading dramatic by using appropriate voices in different parts of the poem.

Use instruments, tape recordings or sound effects made by the children themselves to enhance the presentation.

# 7. Using odd moments

### Age range
Five and upwards.

### Group size
The whole class.

### What you need
No special requirements.

### What to do
There are many times in the day that can easily be allowed to slip, times when children can quickly become boisterous and noisy. Use these moments as opportunities for poems and rhymes.

If the class is working too noisily, start to sing a rhyme with the group you are working with. Soon the whole class will be joining in. When the rhyme has ended the children will usually look at you, waiting expectantly for the next one. In this moment of quiet you can talk to them softly and ask them to talk more quietly.

Other times include:
• the few minutes before play when tidying up is completed;
• when the lesson that you planned took less time than you expected;
• when children are changing for PE;
• after the story and follow-up talk is over;
• when lining up at the door;
• when putting up chairs at the end of the day.

### Further activity
Create your own rhymes for these times, for example, 'This is the way we put up our chairs' to the tune 'Here we go round the mulberry bush'.

# 8. Rhythm of names

### Age range
Six to seven.

### Group size
The whole class or smaller groups.

### What you need
A tambour or a Chinese wood block.

### What to do
Clap the first names of two children whose names have a different syllable count. Talk about the differences with the class.

Use the syllabic count of their first names to make rhythm groups. Ask the children, 'Is your name like this?' and clap a rhythm.

If you have worked on rhythm with your class, they will recognise that different names have long and short syllables. For example:
• — (Paul, Claire, Ben, Ram)
• — – (Megan, Bronwen, Owen, Harjit, Huma)
• — – – (Zobia, Christopher)
• – — – (Zarina, Joanna)
• – – — – (Victoria, Elizabeth)

If that is the case, you can move straight on to play substitution games (see Activity 9, on page 35). If not, take your time working towards this concept before moving on.

### Further activity
Use the syllabic rhythm count with groups of words, such as toys, flowers, clothes, or words connected with the topic you are working on.

the hill...', or '...All the king's horses and all the king's men, *Had scrambled egg for supper* again'. The children will need to listen carefully to identify what you have done, especially if you have only changed one word.

Say the original rhyme, for example 'One, two, buckle my shoe' and let the children join in. Tell them that you want to repeat the rhyme but on your own. This time give a variation on the rhyme, for example:

> One, two, down at the zoo,
> Three, four, fat tigers snore,
> Five, six, monkeys do tricks,
> Seven, eight, pandas sleep
>    late.

After the laughter has died down, ask the children why they were laughing and let them explain to you what you have done. Repeat your version of the rhyme and let the children join in with you as you say it.

Create another version of the original rhyme together. Ask for the children's suggestions for each line, keeping in mind the rhythm of the original. Check the new version for metre by writing the original metre in long and short lines and then writing the new rhythm underneath. Ask questions such as: 'Does it fit exactly?' 'Is there a bit that doesn't fit? Can we use another word instead?'

Write out the poem the children have created and display it for them to read. Try also some of the following suggestions:

## 9. Substitution

### Age range
Six to seven.

### Group size
The whole class or small groups.

### What you need
A tambour or wood block.

### What to do
When children confidently recognise long and short syllables and have worked on Activity 8, begin to work on rhymes, songs and chants. Use the rhythm of a nursery rhyme but substitute the names of children in the class. For example, to the tune of 'Humpty Dumpty':

> Manjit, Sophie, Freddy and
>    Jen,
> Sarah, Charlie, David and
>    Sam....

### Further activity
Make up new verses for other old rhymes, for example, using 'Jack and Jill':

> Ram and Kim went down to
>    town
> To buy a...,
> Ram tripped on a...
> And Kim said....

## 10. Active listening

### Age range
Six or seven and upwards.

### Group size
The whole class or small groups.

### What you need
Rhymes the children know by heart.

### What to do
This activity involves working on a rhyme that the children know very well. Begin to play around with the words of the rhyme in a variety of ways, for example: 'Jack and Jill *ran up*

the original rhyme at the beginning of the booklet and then add the variations.

# 11. Active learning

### Age range
Seven and upwards.

### Group size
The whole class and small groups or pairs.

### What you need
An overhead projector, a transparency of a poem, a copy of the poem for each child, highlighter pens, pencils.

### What to do
Memory activities help to increase the brain's capacity to learn and remember by developing the fine structures of the brain. Therefore, learning poetry by heart allows children to expand their intellect through repetition, but with the added benefit of rhythm and rhyme to help them remember. It also enables them to possess poems and make them their own, and to build up a fund of favourite poems in a pleasurable way.

Do *not* begin this activity by saying 'We are going to learn this poem by heart', as this will put the children off before you even start. Rather, introduce the poem as one you are going to look at closely together.

Display the poem on the overhead projector. If an OHP is not available write out the poem on the chalkboard.

Read the poem through together a couple of times, and then ask the children to read it by themselves. Talk about the meaning of each verse – how

Humpty Dumpty sat on a
wall,
Humpty Dumpty gave a
great ball...
All the king's horses and all
the king's men
Galloped and pranced until
Tuesday at ten.

• Change the pattern of the rhyme, for example:

Humpty Dumpty sat on a
wall
Humpty Dumpty gave a
great shout
All the king's horses and all
the king's men
Tried to discover what it was
about.

## Further activities
• Read to the children some of the regional variations that the Opies found in their research into children's language, rhymes and chants in *The Lore and Language of Schoolchildren* (Paladin), for example, the chant 'Tell tale tit' or the rhyme 'Mary had a little lamb'. See what variations the children can devise.
• Use songs, chants, skipping rhymes, street games and playground games. Work with ones that are familiar to the children.
• Make booklets called 'Variations on a rhyme'. Place

• Leave out rhyming words, for example:

Baa, baa, black sheep
Have you any wool?
Yes sir, yes sir,
Three bags....

• Play around with the words but keep the rhyming pattern, for example:

Meow, meow, black cat
Have you any fur?
Yes indeed sir, and
Three hours of purr;

or:

Sss, sss, grass snake
Have you any skin?
Yes sir, yes sir,
I shed it by the bin.

• Change the words and/or the rhyme, for example:

the poem is developed, key words – linked words, and then read the poem again together.

Move on to discuss with the children which words rhyme, and circle or highlight each rhyme. Read the poem again together, stressing the rhythm and rhyme scheme.

If the poem has more than one verse ask the children if they notice any changes in the chorus line in succeeding verses, and then ask them to repeat the chorus lines with their eyes closed. Having read the poem several times it will be easy for them but it will, nevertheless, come as a surprise to them to know that they have learned, say, a quarter of the poem.

Look at the first verse and point out any repetition, alliteration and assonance, giving each its own mark for identification. Reread the poem aloud, with feeling, after each word search. By this time much of the verse will be known and the children should be able to turn over their copies and say the first verse together. Repeat the process for each verse, and you will find that succeeding verses will be learned quite quickly.

Suggest to the children that they keep their copy of the poem in their pocket or school bag, so that they can glance at it whenever they like and try to say it from memory. If they become stuck on a word, tell them to think through the poem, rather than turn to the copy straight away. This way the word will generally surface.

Waiting times, such as waiting for a lesson or programme to start, waiting for a bus or waiting to go to sleep, are all times when poems can be said in the head or allowed to drift through the mind.

## Further activities
Once the children have learned this technique they can work together in pairs or small groups to learn poems.

Some useful poems include:
• 'Wishes' (Anon) in *The Oxford Treasury of Children's Poems* (Oxford University Press);
• 'The Owl and the Pussy-cat' by Edward Lear, in *The Oxford Treasury of Children's Poems*;
• 'Hurt no living thing' by Christina Rossetti, in *The Oxford Treasury of Children's Poems*;
• 'Rice Pudding' by A. A. Milne, in *When We Were Very Young* (Methuen).

# 12. Introducing a poem

## Age range
Seven and upwards.

## Group size
The whole class.

## What you need
A good supply of poetry and rhyme books suited to the children's age group – see the Bibliography on page 171.

## What to do
Introduce at least one short poem or rhyme every day or two every other day. Talk about the topic of the poem before you read it so that children have a basic understanding on which to focus their listening. Choose a poem linked with a current task, a topic, a story, the weather, a toy or an experience that will be familiar to the children.

The first time you read it, say nothing. Let it sink in for a minute and then read it again.

After the second reading talk about the poem to encourage active listening and to get the children thinking about what they are hearing. Was the poem sad or happy? Was it serious or funny? Did it tell a story, or describe something? Was it a joke, a tongue-twister? Leave any further work on the poem for another session.

## Further activity

Next time you read the poem read it twice. Then ask the children what it made them think about. What did they like or dislike about it? How did it make them feel?

On another occasion, ask if there could have been any further verses. If so, what might these be about? Don't ask closed questions (those with yes or no answers); ask open questions so that the children have a chance to express their thoughts and the ideas that the poem may have given rise to.

# 13. Working orally on a poem

### Age range
Seven and upwards.

### Group size
The whole class or small groups.

### What you need
A large sheet of paper with the poem written on it.

### What to do
Read the poem to the children twice, and then decide if you want them to explore the poem in greater depth.

You may find it helpful, certainly with the younger children, to put up the copy of the poem before you begin to talk about it. With older children it is often a good idea to talk about the impressions they have drawn from the poem before they see it in front of them, although they will need to see a copy of the poem in order to talk about its form. Use open-ended questions similar to the following, adapting them as appropriate to your class and the poem.

### Language
• What words stand out for you?
• What effect do they have?
• Would you have used different words?
• Why?

### Content
• What do you think the poem is about?
• What is the writer saying?

### Feelings
• How does the poem make you feel?
• What is its message to you?
• Does it change how you feel?
• Do you feel the same way as the poet about this, or are your views different?

### The poem
• What is its message to you?
• How does it achieve this?
• Does it work, as a poem?

### Form
• How are the words laid out?
• Is there a shape to the poem?
• How would you describe the way the poem looks?
• How is it different from prose?

# 14. Your own collection

### Age range
Adults.

### What you need
Poems, paper, pens, crayons, a file (preferably a ring-binder), clear plastic wallets, steel pins, mounts.

### What to do
Create your own anthology from the poems you have shared with the children and those they have shared with you. Arrange the poems in subject or topic groups. Make a bibliography, source and resource list at the back of the book for reference purposes.

Type up each poem and annotate it so that it is ready for reading. Make notes of the date you used it and how you presented it at the bottom. Comment on the things that worked well, or otherwise, and make suggestions for improving the presentation next time.

Make a top copy for display purposes and place the annotated copy behind it in a clear plastic wallet. It makes a very attractive collection to share if you write and illustrate the poems yourself.

Teach yourself simple calligraphy. It doesn't take long with a good instruction manual, and if, like me, you are less than happy with the quality of your illustrations there are a number of books on the market that contain borders, layouts and designs on which you can mount your work.

Clear plastic pockets will keep your sheets fresh, clean and undamaged. They will also make it easier for children to read through your anthology and see how it is put together.

If you write your poems in a landscape rather than portrait format on A4 or A5 paper you can keep each poem in a wallet and use the eyelets to pin it up on the wall. Always use fine steel pins (lills) not ugly drawing pins.

Keep a collection of mounts, cut 4cm longer and wider than A4 or A5, to place behind a poem when pinning it up. These coloured mounts can then be used several times over.

# CHAPTER 3

# Ways of getting started

Graham Wallas (1858–1932) wrote: 'The little girl had the making of a poet in her who, being told to be sure of her meaning before she spoke, said "How can I know what I think until I see what I say?"' (The Art of Thought).

The little girl is right. We do need to get our thoughts down on paper to consider them and put them in the best order. Children need to be able to set down what is in their heads and then make decisions about it without having to be overly concerned in the first stage about the final product.

Poetry is a way of extending knowledge. It can help us to become aware of issues and events or to escape from them. It may help us to see humour or present us with the darker side of life. Sometimes in 'seeing what we say', we find out things we didn't know we knew. This is no less true for children. Their ideas tend to be concrete, since the majority of primary children have yet to acquire the ability to make and handle abstractions.

# BACKGROUND

This chapter looks at different ways of beginning, of getting words down on paper, of seeing what we know and think. What is written may or may not be a poem; that is a decision to be made once the words are down. A poem should not be forced. It may be better to use the words as the hook on which to hang a story. But whether the writing is prose or poetry it is getting started that matters.

## Preparing to start

We all need help in getting started. A blank page can often appear very daunting and it takes time and practice to be able to pick up a sheet of paper and start to write straight away.

Make it easier for children to start by having an area in the classroom where writing materials are kept and, close by, a work table equipped for presenting and mounting work. In the writing area provide a supply of different types of paper – rough, blank and best quality. Provide lined paper to go underneath blank paper and see that there are pencils, crayons, felt-tipped pens, ink pens, italic pens and inks of different colours to choose from.

On the work table have a trimmer, adhesive, spreaders, needles and button thread for making books, card and mounting paper of different colours and sizes. Teach children to save offcuts, as these can often be used as backings for short poems, for labels in anthologies, or for topic work.

Draw up a rota of children to take charge of these areas, checking that the pencils are sharp, that the pens work and that there are plenty of materials. The adhesive pots will also need to be kept filled. Use small ones with lids, which can be filled from a five-litre container. If you spread a little Vaseline around the edge of the container and the screw top there will not be a problem getting the lid off.

To avoid queues, noise and 'Please Miss, what do we do next?', have a tray where the children can leave any work they want you to look at if you are busy. It is important, however, to look at the work as often as you can. Put up a list

for the children to sign if they need to see you. Having signed up, the children should keep on trying unless they are really stuck, in which case they can get on with something else until you are free. Therefore, make sure that they always have plenty of work to get on with. With older children, lists help you to keep track of who you have seen and when, how much help a particular child needs and how that child is progressing.

Make sure that the children are clear about what they have to do. Discuss with them what you want them to do if:
• they get stuck;
• they need a listening ear to try something out;
• they have finished;
• they cannot spell a word.

## Brainstorming

Poems are made out of words, carefully chosen and used sparingly. Children need to have a reservoir of words from which to select in order to find the ones that are exactly right

for their needs. Words can be collected in a number of ways, but the following have been found to be most useful with primary children.
• Making a collection of words related to a topic brings out some words which may well have been forgotten. We usually know far more words than we use in our day-to-day vocabulary. These are unlikely to be brought forward without concentrated dredging. Talking about a topic, exploring feelings and senses and writing lists of words or phrases all help this to happen.
• Streams of consciousness are ways of getting thoughts and ideas down on paper quickly, before they are forgotten. There is no need to be overly concerned about spelling,

handwriting or punctuation, but what is written must be legible and comprehensible.
• Lists of different kinds all help to focus the children's minds, to bring to the forefront words they may have heard, read or seen, but not used for some time. If it is possible, try to let the children experience different situations, such as an autumn walk, so that they can find out for themselves what happens when they scuff

through dried leaves. Let them pick them up, feel their texture, throw a handful up in the air and see what happens. When you get back to the classroom, write the words 'autumn leaves' on the board and surround it with all the words the children think of in connection with how they felt on the walk.

Younger children should create their lists with you, and then as they gain more experience they can work in small groups. Older children, however, should be able to write their lists at the same time as you do. Ask the children to identify words they have included that are different from the words on your list.

## Getting started

There are a number of different ways of helping children to start writing. Using starter lines is one way. This means that children are not faced with a dauntingly blank page but with a 'working document'. With words there already to act as a trigger to the mind, other words will follow more readily. Other starters include discussion, using pictures, posters, photographs, titles, cards and direct experience.

## Feelings

Children have strong feelings about the people, creatures and objects with which they come into contact. Adults usually learn to suppress and control these feelings, so art attempts to break through the systems of habit and well-ordered sentiment, and bring back a little of the fire, the passion and the expression of feeling for some object, creature, person or event which we might otherwise take for granted.

# ACTIVITIES

## 1. Beginning lists

### Age range
Five to six.

### Group size
The whole class or small groups.

### What you need
A flipchart, large sheets of paper or chalkboard, felt-tipped pens or chalk.

### What to do
Lists are useful ways of focusing thoughts. Choose something related to current work, such as fire, water, food, pets, transport, wheels and so on. Draw an appropriate outline, for example, a bonfire complete with flames and smoke or an ice-cream cone. Ask the children for words that the picture makes them think of and write these in the picture. For example, fill the flames with words like red, orange, bright, hot, warm, smell, smoke, sticks and so on.

Surround the picture with any interesting phrases the children may say such as, 'I hate the smoke, it makes me cough'; 'The heat made my cheeks on fire'; 'In the morning the fire looked grey and dead but it was still hot underneath'; 'We cooked some potatoes in the fire'. Write them all down, filling the paper with the children's words and ideas, because it is from these that the poem will be created.

Go through the words and phrases on the sheet and write 'I see' on a second sheet. Ask the children to tell you the phrases connected with seeing. Ask them what else they can see in the bonfire and write these phrases underneath. On a third sheet of paper write 'I hear' and proceed in the same way. You should judge whether or not it is appropriate to take this work any further. The children may be ready to go on or it may be better to come back to it after a change of activity. However, aim to make sheets representing all the senses.

### Further activities
Return to the 'I see' sheet. Reorder the phrases to give cohesion and do some simple editing to keep the basic pulse of each phrase constant. Read it through together and decide whether to leave in the words 'I see' or remove them. Do the same with the other sheets.

Having completed all five 'verses', look at the length of each one, adding or removing lines so that the poem is balanced.

Write up the resulting piece of work and display it with other topic-related work.

## 2. Things you see and hear

### Age range
Five and upwards.

### Group size
The whole class or small groups.

### What you need
The poem 'Dog in the playground' by Allan Ahlberg, in *Please Mrs Butler* (Puffin); children's own pictures, photographs, posters or illustrations of an active scene; a flipchart or large sheet of paper, felt-tipped pens, pencils, paper, crayons.

### What to do
Read the poem 'Dog in the playground' together and talk about it. Have the children experienced something like this? Ask them to draw a picture of something similar that happened to them. Tell them to make it a busy scene with lots of things going on.

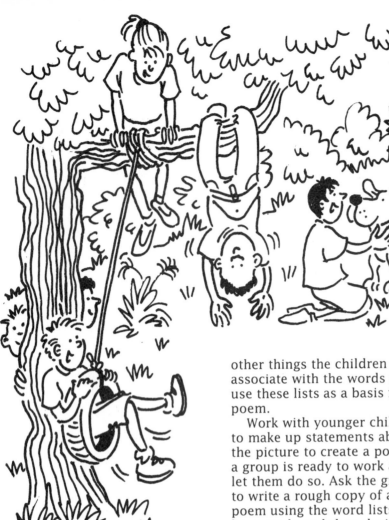

Use one of the children's pictures or one from your collection and talk about all the things that are happening in it. If the children were there, what would they see and hear? Fold a piece of paper in four, lengthways, and head the first column 'see' and the third 'hear'. List the things the children would see and hear under the two headings.

Go over each list together and write in the second and fourth columns any descriptive words that each word brings to mind. Add any feelings or other things the children associate with the words and use these lists as a basis for a poem.

Work with younger children to make up statements about the picture to create a poem. If a group is ready to work alone let them do so. Ask the group to write a rough copy of a poem using the word lists they have made and then decide on the form most suited to what they have to say.

## Further activity
The children can illustrate their work or make a collage.

# 3. Stream of consciousness

## Age range
Six to eight.

## Group size
Pairs or individuals.

## What you need
Pencils, paper, scissors, coloured pencils.

## What to do
Talk about a chosen topic with the children and ask them to write down everything they can think of to do with the topic. Tell them not to worry about the order of the ideas, the spelling or their handwriting (so long as the writing is legible). Each thought must be written on a separate line. Give them five minutes in which to do this task.

Ask the children to share with the rest of the class what they have written. Any ideas the children pick up on from hearing others read their work can be added to their own lists.

Tell the children to cut up their lists and group similar ideas together. They can tap out the syllables in each line to find the pulse and then work on the lines to try to make the number of beats constant.

Bring the class back together so that they can share their writing with each other. Use this time as an opportunity to show them how to look at the writing of others and suggest ways in which to offer ideas and criticisms in a constructive manner.

## Further activity
Where appropriate ask the children to write out and illustrate their poem for presentation.

# 4. Day-dreams

### Age range
Six to eight.

### Group size
Younger children will need to work as a whole class, but others can work in small groups or pairs.

### What you need
Pencils, paper.

### What to do
The following day-dream rhymes were written by eight-year-olds:

> My Mum thinks I'm just lazy
> when I'm lying on my bed,
> but really I'm a highwayman
> with a price upon my head.
>
> My teacher thinks I'm
>    reading
> when my head's deep in a
>    book,
> but really I'm a pirate
> with a black patch and a
>    hook.

Tell the children they are going to create day-dream rhymes, following the same format as the poems above. They should think of ideas to fill in the gaps in the following phrase:
'My... thinks I'm... when... but really...'.

They can then edit and redraft their lines so that they produce a short poem.

## Further activity
More verses can be added to these poems, exploring the day-dream further. The last verse should be a reprise or variation of the first one.

# 5. Mini-thesaurus

### Age range
Six and upwards.

### Group size
The whole class, pairs or individuals.

### What you need
A flipchart and felt-tipped pens or a chalkboard and chalk, pencil, paper.

### What to do
Make a list of words associated directly with the topic. For example, if the topic is football, use words like kick, boots, ball, pass, goal.

With younger children start by working together on a chalkboard or flipchart. Write the topic name at the top of the board or draw a large outline symbolising the topic, for example, a football, and fill the inside with topic words.

Use these words to develop descriptive phrases from which a poem can be created.

After working a few times in this way most of the children will be ready to work in pairs or small groups to write their own mini-thesaurus. Limit the time for the task to about five minutes at this age.

Older children can work on their own. Ask them to write their words as a list in two minutes. They can then compare lists and use them as a basis for a poem.

### Further activity

Use the lists to write poems. Read out list poems such as 'The fight of the Year' by Roger McGough from *Go and Open the Door*, edited by Moira Andrew (Macmillan).

# 6. Questions, questions

### Age range

Six and upwards.

### Group size

The whole class or groups.

### What you need

The poem 'Inquisitiveness' by Colin West from *Not to be Taken Seriously* (Hutchinson), a flipchart or a large sheet of paper, felt-tipped pens, pencils, paper.

### What to do

From about four years of age children start to ask questions like 'Why is the sky blue?', 'What is a rainbow?', 'Where does the rain go?' and 'Why does a puddle get smaller?'.

Read 'Inquisitiveness' to the children. Ask them about the kinds of questions they ask, and write these on a large sheet of paper. Three questions will be enough to start with, but leave plenty of space under each question.

Use a felt-tipped pen of a different colour from the questions and make up, with the children, a number of answers to each question. Select from the answers the ones that fit the rhythm best, and edit the questions and answers as necessary.

Older children will be able to work in groups. Ask them to work out some questions together and then individually write some responses. Then they can put their answers together and use them as a basis for their poem.

### Further activity

Write up Colin West's poem and mount the children's work round it.

# 7. Group poems

### Age range

Seven to nine.

### Group size

Four or six.

### What you need

Card, felt-tipped pens, a box, paper, adhesive, scissors.

### What to do

Write out a number of starter lines on to card, for example:
• I went to bed late last night because...;
• My arm is in a sling because...;
• I didn't finish my work because...;
• I forgot my plimsolls because...;
• Holidays are great because...;
• I won't go past the empty house because....

Put all these cards into a lucky-dip box and ask one child from each group to choose a card from the box. Each child in the group must then try to write three or four ideas for finishing the sentence.

All the sentences from the group should then be cut into strips and put in the best possible order, paying attention to the endings of each line. The lines may become progressively more

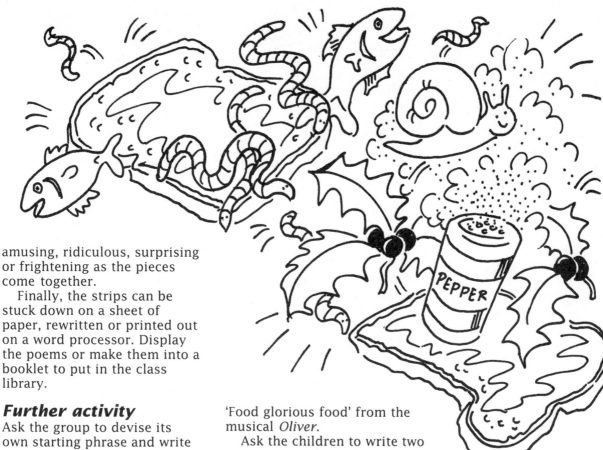

amusing, ridiculous, surprising or frightening as the pieces come together.

Finally, the strips can be stuck down on a sheet of paper, rewritten or printed out on a word processor. Display the poems or make them into a booklet to put in the class library.

### Further activity
Ask the group to devise its own starting phrase and write a poem from it. The new starting phrase can then also be added to the lucky dip.

## 8. Sandwich fillings

### Age range
Seven to nine.

### Group size
Pairs or individuals.

### What you need
Pencils, paper, a tape recorder, a recording of 'Food glorious food'.

### What to do
Have a class discussion about food. Ask the children what they like and what they really hate to eat. Play a recording of 'Food glorious food' from the musical *Oliver*.

Ask the children to write two poems – one about the most delicious sandwich they have ever eaten and the other about the most horrible one. These could be either based on a real-life experience or pure fantasy!

The children can then use the first line: The most delicious sandwich I have ever eaten had...' to write a poem about it. They can substitute the word 'horrible' for 'delicious' for the second time.

### Further activities
Ask the children to make a collage of a giant sandwich. The filling could be shown protruding out of the sandwich, or they could show the sandwich exploding and casting out its evil contents! The children's poems should then be displayed along with their pictures.

## 9. Openings

### Age range
Seven and upwards.

### Group size
Pairs or individuals.

### What you need
Pencils, large pieces of paper, crayons, scissors, adhesive, card.

### What to do
Ask the children to draw a door, a gateway, a window with curtains, an Easter egg, a cake and a flower. When they have finished they should cut through the middle of each one to make an opening. For the

door and gateway the children may prefer to give each one a handle and cut round it so that it opens as a normal door or gateway.

The children should then write a list of words and phrases evoked by each picture, using a stream of consciousness or mini-thesaurus technique (see pages 46 and 47).

From these lists the children can write a poem. When they have completed the editing they should mount the relevant picture on to card and write the poem behind the opening.

# 10. Catalogue poems

### Age range
Seven and upwards.

### Group size
Small groups or pairs.

### What you need
Pencils, paper, *You Can't Catch Me* by Michael Rosen (Puffin), a tape recorder, a tape of Flanders and Swann's 'The gas man cometh'.

### What to do
Read the rhymes 'This is the house that Jack built' and Michael Rosen's 'This is the hand' in *You Can't Catch Me*. Play Michael Flanders and Donald Swann's recording of 'The gas man cometh' which is in a similar style.

Talk about the way these poems are sequenced and discuss other suitable subjects for such a poem, for example 'This is the nose that...' or 'This is the brain that...'.

Make a list with the children of all the things the chosen subject can do, both reasonable and fantastic, and use them as a list as a basis for creating a catalogue poem.

### Further activity
Put up a picture of what the chosen subject (nose, brain or whatever) and mount the children's poem around it. This could then be the starting point for a topic.

# 11. I feel...

### Age range
Seven and upwards.

### Group size
Pairs or individuals.

### What you need
Pencils, paper, scissors, adhesive.

### What to do
Ask the children about the different types of feelings they have experienced at one time or another. They will probably tell you that there are times when they feel embarrassed, sad, happy, giggly, afraid, guilty and so on. Ask them about these feelings, when and why they get them and what they can do about them. Make a list of the different kinds of feelings they have.

Now make a list of beginnings:
• I get...
• I am...
• I feel...
• It is...
• When I....

Ask the children to choose a beginning and a feeling and combine them to give them a first line of a poem, for example: 'I get upset when...' or 'I am sad when...' and so on.

The children should then write all the different ways they experience that emotion to complete the line.

When the children have written four or five lines, ask them to look at the rhythm of each line and edit the lines to keep the rhythm constant, rearranging them as necessary. If the children have written more than four or five lines, ask them to rearrange them in clusters to give the piece cohesion.

Create a wall display of the children's poems. However, some children may not want to share their inner feelings and it is important that you respect their wish for privacy. In an atmosphere of trust, this will usually change eventually.

### Further activity
Another way of using this idea is to start the first three lines in the same way, but using the reverse feeling for the fourth line, for example:

I feel sad when...
I feel sad when...
I feel sad when...
but I feel happy when....

## 12. Pattern poems

### Age range
Seven and upwards.

### Group size
Small groups or pairs.

### What you need
Pencils, paper.

### What to do
Read, discuss and display traditional rhymes like:
- 'Monday's child';
- 'Solomon Grundy';
- 'January brings the snow';
- 'One for sorrow';
- 'Cherry stones'.

In the same category as these is A. A. Milne's 'When I was One' in *Now We Are Six* (my hand-me-down copy is Methuen 1928, but there are newer editions!)

Ask the children to make up their own rhymes based on numbers, days or months. They should start each line with a number, day or month and then construct a rhyme following a similar pattern to one of the traditional poems.

### Further activity
Ask the children to search for other similar pattern poems and make an anthology.

## 13. Two sides of a coin

### Age range
Seven and upwards.

### Group size
Pairs or individuals.

### What you need
Pencils, paper.

### What to do
There are two sides to every coin. We like people when they behave in a way that pleases us and dislike them when they behave in a way we dislike or disapprove of. Similarly we can be happy or sad, glad or sorry about the things we, and others, say and do.

Talk about this with the children. What do they like about their parents, brother, sister or friend?

Ask them to write three things they like about one of these people and then one thing they do not like. They should try to write concise statements, but they don't have to attempt to make them rhyme, for example:

I like you when...
I like you when...
I like you when...
but I don't like you when....

Working this way encourages children to look for the good in people. It is so easy to put others down, but it is also important to be able to accept an honest comment between friends. This can happen if it is said in the right spirit. Writing three positives, but only one negative accentuates this positive approach.

# 14. Pick a card

### Age range
Seven and upwards.

### Group size
Small groups, pairs or individuals.

### What you need
Card, pencils, paper.

### What to do
Make a collection of cards with titles on them, such as:
• Wellington boots;
• A door marked private;
• Cats;
• A bridge;
• Favourite things;
• The alien;
• New shoes;
• Green eyes;
• Bare trees;
• Mud;
• Voices;
• Night.

Keep these cards in a box. To use them take out a number of cards and place them face down on the table so that the children can choose a card. Once they have picked a card the children need to focus their thinking carefully using word lists of different kinds, brainstorming, streams of consciousness, links with the five senses, word associations, alliteration, assonance and descriptive phrases.

The children can then select, from the lists that they compile, the words and phrases that appeal to them. From these words and any further ideas they may spark off, the poem can then be created.

As the children are introduced to different kinds of poems they will also be able to select the style they want to use for their poems.

### Further activities
• After writing one poem the children may like to try using another style to represent their ideas.
• The children could do the same activity, but using various artefacts and pictures instead of cards.

# 15. Anything you can do...

### Age range
Seven and upwards.

### Group size
Small groups or pairs.

### What you need
Tape recorder, a tape of a popular song, pencils, paper.

### What to do
Choose a song which children will respond well to. It may be a song that is currently in vogue, but this is not essential. For example, 'Anything you can do' from *Annie Get Your Gun* is an old song, but it has a theme that children can relate to.

Play the song two or three times to the children and talk about it with them. If you are using 'Anything you can do', ask them to list the things they can do better than another person. Once they have completed their lists they should swap them with a partner and respond to each other's lists. The resultant challenge and response lists can then be turned into a poem or an adaptation of the song.

Not all songs are suitable for this activity, but often the title can spark off ideas for poems, for example, 'Memory' from *Cats*, or 'Yesterday' by the Beatles. If you use 'Yesterday', the children could list all the things that might have happened and create rhyming couplets. They might add a chorus such as 'Oh what a rotten yesterday'.

### Further activity
Play 'Homeward bound' by Simon and Garfunkel. How would the children feel if they were prevented from going home? After discussing the song they can write down their feelings. These can then be turned into a poem.

# 16. Battle lines

### Age range
Eight and upwards.

### Group size
Groups of eight.

### What you need
A flipchart or chalkboard, felt-tipped pens, chalk, pencils, paper.

### What to do
Ask the children to tell you the things they feel strongly about and write them on the board. Subjects might include worms, spiders, ice-cream, tidying bedrooms, going to bed, television, pocket money and so on.

Each group should then choose a subject from the list. They should then divide themselves into two teams of four and one team must write about the things they like, and the other the things they hate about the subject. For example:
• What I hate about...is...
• What I like about...is
or more directly:
• I hate... because...
• I like... because....

Each team should write an agreed number of lines (between four and eight), and once they have done this, the group as a whole should look at ways of marrying the like and hate lines.

The poem can be written in alternating lines or couplets for and against, or in groups of verses in favour followed by verses against. The object is to form a harmonious sequence, perhaps starting with minor points and gradually moving to the more important ones.

# 17. Reflections

### Age range
Eight and upwards.

### Group size
Small groups, pairs or individuals.

### What you need
Pencils, paper.

### What to do
Read the children some poems like 'The End' ('When I was One...') by A. A. Milne from *Now We Are Six* (Methuen) or 'I remember, I remember,' by Thomas Hood.

Talk to the children about:
• things they remember;
• things they wish for;
• things they cannot forget;
• what they could do when they were small;
• what they can do now.

In other words, get them to reflect upon their own lives.

Put up a series of starter lines for the children to select from, for example;
• I remember...;
• Sometimes I wish...;
• I can't forget...;
• When I was little I... but now I'm older I....

The children can use one of these phrases to start each line or stanza, or just for the beginning of the poem.

### Further activity
Use sayings as starter lines, such as:
• You'll never believe this but...;
• Look at the way they...;
• I'm glad I have....
The children will have suggestions for other sayings to add to yours. Make a collection of them and add others as you hear them.

## 18. Who's doing what?

### Age range
Eight and upwards.

### Group size
Small groups or pairs.

### What you need
Pencils, paper, poems which describe a complicated scene.

### What to do
Read some poems like Wes Magee's 'Morning break' in *All the Day Through* (Evans).

Choose an event or location where people are likely to be involved in a number of different activities, such as the playground, the seaside, sports day, a festival, getting changed for PE, a show. Discuss the situation with the children and together build up a verbal picture of all the things that are or could be happening there. Ask questions like:
• Who might be there?
• What might they be doing?
• Why?
Each group should then choose a name, a verb and an action from that list to make each line into a short rhyme. The character may have a first name and a family name, as in Wes Magee's poem, or merely a first name, for example:

Niki's giving filthy looks,
Amram sits and stares,
Harjit searches for her socks
Tracey stamps and glares.

After writing a number of four-lined verses, the children should end their poems with a line to identify the location or activity being carried out in the poem, for example:

What a silly carry on
Changing for PE!

### Further activities
• Copy out the original poem and display the children's poems around it.
• Ask the children to copy their poems into their own anthologies (see Chapter 4).
• Use a photograph or picture of a scene and ask the groups to write a poem about it in a similar way.

# CHAPTER 4

# *Processes*

Ovid wrote: 'Of its own accord my song would come in the right rhythms, and what I was trying to say was poetry' (Tristia).

However, we are not all so fortunate. We often struggle to achieve even the simplest verse. In some ways children are freer, less confined by the strictures of adulthood and conditioning. We must be wary that while teaching the skills and processes involved in writing genres, we do not take this freedom away from them.

# BACKGROUND

## What skills?

There is no correct method of teaching poetry, but children do need to be taught to behave like real writers, getting the ideas down first, then rewriting them clearly and presenting them in an interesting and appropriate way.

To become proficient in any craft you have to learn certain skills. You do not become a photographer merely by using the 'point and click' method, even with the most sophisticated of modern cameras. You have to know about aperture, depth of field, shutter speed, the effect of light and colour, composition, the attributes of the many films available and so on.

Similarly, there are a number of skills and techniques to be learned and practised before you are able to use written language effectively. You need to learn how to make words say what you want them to say, in the genre that is right for the purpose. Your message needs to be written in legible writing using the correct spelling, and punctuation that makes the meaning clear.

A tall order, especially when applied to poetry. But before children can develop the skills of rhyme and metrical pattern they have to learn these more basic ones:
• to observe;
• to get words down on paper;
• to redraft a first copy;
• to present it suitably.
These are the skills that will be covered in this chapter.

## How do you write?

Many teachers ask children to do what they, themselves, rarely if ever do – write a poem. If you don't write yourself, how can you know what it is like and where the problems may lie? If you do not know the processes involved, how can you be expected to help the children?

Whatever writing we ask children to do, we should work alongside them, at least some of the time, reading and presenting our work along with theirs.

One of the advantages of working with the children is that you get involved in writing and so give the children the freedom to work on their own or, if they are stuck, time to retrieve themselves rather than being dependent on you. Another advantage is that you come to understand the writing process more fully.

When you are helping the children you cannot work on your own poem to the same degree. Make time to work on it later in the day. Next morning say 'Last night I was working on the poem I started with you yesterday...', then talk about the changes you have made, and why you made them, showing the children the drafts. Tell them whether you think the poem is finished or whether you will want to work on it some more. This will help the children to gain insight into the way a poem is worked on and to learn how to make it tighter, making the adjectives work and choosing words with care.

## Processes

What are the writing processes we go through? This is a difficult question to answer because we have each to find our own method, pattern or style. Even if we do have our own way of working, this may change from time to time or from piece to piece. What we need to do is to show children how to take their rough piece of work and make alterations

to that, hone it into shape and arrive at a final version from which they may or may not make a fair copy. Thus they learn the route and, with practice and experience, will develop a style that suits them.

Writing is best done in two stages. The first is concerned with fluency, shape and cohesion – starting the initial flow, getting ideas down on paper and working them into a coherent and cohesive shape. The second is concerned with refining, editing and presenting the poem.

## Stage one

### The spark or stimulus
The stimulus that sparks off a poem can be almost anything. It can be an artefact, a visit, an experience, a piece of music, a picture, a person, a treasure, a pet or a spider's web 'bedewed with diamonds'. Inspiration may come from looking at a perfectly ordinary thing in a completely different way.

Most of us go around with our eyes blinkered. We do not see, we merely look. We need to teach children to observe, and we can do this by encouraging them to:
• make observational drawings;
• attend to details;
• use their senses to find out about things;
• ask questions and seek answers.

### Getting it down
The most important thing is to get down on paper what you want to say, in words charged with the utmost possible meaning.

The first draft of a piece should aim to get the ideas down, quickly before they slip away, while the thoughts, ideas and words flow; jotting down suitable words, phrases and rhymes as they come to mind. Surface areas can be sorted out later.

Start your own writing at the same time as the children. This gives the children time to start, and you won't jump in too soon. After about five or ten minutes begin to walk around quietly so as not to disturb their concentration.

Help them if they are really stuck or unsure how to go forward. Sometimes the children will need time to think.

When discussing the children's work with them, comment positively. Make remarks like 'That's a good start' and 'You've some good ideas here'.

Help them to move on by asking appropriate questions:
• 'What happened next?'
• 'How did you or it see/feel/ touch/think?'
• 'What other things do you want to say?'
• 'Did you want to say anything about...?'

If they are obviously struggling, suggest they start again, but in a different way. They could also look at the way another child has begun the poem, or look at the class anthologies for ideas. Having physically moved away from the difficulty and seen other poems they will put their worries into perspective, and with new ideas in their heads, make a fresh start.

Do not worry over-much about spelling and handwriting initially, *but* the writing must be legible. Poor writing habits should never be encouraged and if work is continually written carelessly then children's handwriting rapidly deteriorates. In addition, work that is written carelessly ceases to be valued by either the reader or the writer.

*The Slimy Toad*

At the bottom of a deep, slithery
well,
Beneath a lumpy, wet
Underneath thorrible rock
drip
Where the water went drip ʌ
drip all day
Sat a

### Words

We want children to use the words which are closest to the meanings they want to convey. They need to enlarge their vocabulary, and we will look at various ways of doing this in Chapter 6.

### The genre

At some point the question has to be asked: 'What is the best form to convey what I want to say?'

The genre, whether free verse, rhyme or metre, poetry or prose, is decided by the style or content of the piece. It also depends, largely, on the writer's interpretation of the subject and her experience of what will suit it best.

## Stage two

### Revising and redrafting

What we are asking children to do when they redraft a poem is to take a second look at it and make a further version of their writing. We want them to look closely at what they have written, to ask the question, 'Does it say what I want it to say in the way that I want to say it?' Redrafting requires of them a high level of concentration, in order to crystalise what they wish to express. It is better that they write ten tight lines than ten times as many filled with a verbal mishmash.

Children can cut their writing and abandon great chunks of it to create something that is tight, succinct and apposite. We want them to work on it until they are satisfied with the new or revised version of the poem.

If the concept of redrafting is well established at primary level, it becomes a natural part of the writing process. As a result, children not only become more critical of their own work and that of others, but also develop an awareness of what makes good writing.

But let's not get too carried away by the need to redraft; not all writing needs to be changed. Sometimes writing needs to be left just as it is, whether it is a stream of outpourings or something that came right, straight off the pen, first time.

### Editing

Working on the final copy to make it ready for publication or presentation is called editing. This task will include further deletion of extraneous words or phrases, exchanging words for others which are more apposite, making images more striking, and cutting and splicing lines to tighten the poem. It will also include adjusting the spelling, punctuation and grammar and deciding the way the final copy is to be presented.

At about the age of seven children can begin to edit their own writing, taking it on a stage further from redrafting. Teach them the editing markings that you use; for example:

• a question mark over words that do not seem quite right;
• a wiggly line under words whose spelling is suspect;
• // where a new line should start;
• a circle around words to be moved and an arrow to where they should be transferred;
• ∧ for words omitted, which should be written above. (Missing phrases may need to be written in the margin and linked with a line to the arrowhead.)

Devise a check card that relates to a particular activity that the children are working on. Write clearly the editing marks you want the children to use and suggest ways that they can work through their drafts.

### Conferencing

Conferencing can involve talking with a child about his or her work for a brief moment, or for a longer session, looking closely at the poem. Sessions should not last too long and one is rarely enough.

Ask the children to read through their work two or three times before coming to a conference with you. They can ask a friend to read it through too, or put the writing away and revise it later. It is important that when the children come to conferencing they have already given their work a close look.

Put up a piece of A4 paper, with the day's date on it, and ask the children to sign up when they want a conference. Tick the names of the children after conferencing with them, and use the sheet to update your records.

My record sheets list the names of each pupil down the left-hand side and the titles of the pieces of work in question across the top. In the columns is written the date, with symbols to show the stage the work is at, for example:
• R = rough copy;
• D = draft (1, 2 or 3);
• E = edited;
• F = finished.

This method makes it easy to keep track of who has been seen, when, for what purpose and where they are in their assignments.

Make yourself a place where you can talk quietly with children, whether about work or about personal concerns. Sit side by side so you can both see the child's work. Always ask, 'May I read through your work before we talk about it?' and do so, don't just skim it.

Give the work back to the child before you start to work on it together, so that the child keeps ownership of the work.

What are you looking for in a child's writing? Perhaps imagery that is fresh and original; a feeling of tension and energy; an internal rhythm that tells you the writing could not be prose; a unity of thought and feeling, word and rhythm? No child's work is ever completely bad. Look for the good – you'll always find something.

The way of working with each child, the kind of questions you ask, will help them to appraise their own

work and that of others. Always be constructive in your comments and criticisms. Three praises for each criticism is the maxim to work by when talking with children about their writing. If they have not yet written anything down ask them to tell you about the idea that they can think of most clearly.

You need to give the child all of your attention so that you can follow where he leads. He must decide the path the writing will take, but you can make suggestions. It is not always easy to see where one's own writing is leading;

sometimes one is too close to it. Listen carefully to what the child wants to achieve, give opinions, and ask the kind of leading questions that will help him see a way out of an impasse. Be prepared to give him time to absorb what you have said and its implications.

The first conference will be a thoughtful assessment of the content. Tell the child what it is you like about the poem. Statements like 'Oh, that's lovely dear', 'Good', or just 'Well done', tell the child nothing of real value. Don't talk down to them, credit them with what they can do. Praise with specific comments like:
• 'I like the way you have used this word.'
• 'The rhythm carries me along.'
• 'The powerful description in that line forms a vivid picture in my mind.'
• 'I like the way you've used this group of words.'
• 'The ending makes me think again about what your poem is saying.'

Ask questions like:
• 'What do you mean by this word?'
• 'What is 'nice' about it?'
• 'What kind of sound did it make?'
• 'How did it move?'
• 'Can you say more about...?'

In subsequent conferences, the technical aspects can be assessed. The children can also form groups to hold conferences about each other's poems. By discussing their work with each other and seeking opinions, children are helped to develop a critical awareness which will assist them in their own writing.

Before letting the children work in groups, ask them to work as a class on one of your poems or on a poem written by one of them. This will help to guide their thoughts in the right channels.

When the children go into their groups, one child should read out his poem while the others listen. They should concentrate on the imagery and on the inner rhythm of the piece. It may help them to have a copy each. The children can then work as a group to offer constructive criticism to the poet.

### Marking
Marking is taking a lead pencil and annotating the text, not slashing it with a blood-red ball-point pen! The object of

marking is to *improve*, not *reprove*. Always look for as much good as you can before noting weak points. The way we mark a child's work has direct bearing on what will be offered to us next time. We want to help the children to surmount their difficulties, not wallow in them; to help them develop new strategies, not shy away, anxious and afraid to try for fear of getting it wrong.

The vital parts of a poem are its use of imagery, tension, rhythm, its wholeness, shape, form and the use and order of words. Poetry is not about facts. What we look for is a totality which enables us to recreate or relive the experience; precise adjectives which empower nouns to make descriptions vivid, active verbs that bring drama to a poem which develops logically and consistently. This is what we are leading children towards when we mark their poems.

Develop a consistent style of marking so that the children quickly recognise what you mean.
• Tick words you like, images that appeal and ideas that have depth.
• Put a question mark over words that are weak or inappropriate, or that have been repeated unnecessarily.

• Draw a wiggly line under words that have been misspelled.
• Mark // where a new line should start.
• Circle punctuation errors according to your expectations of the child.

Always let a child know what you think of her work. Write comments in the margin or at the end of the piece as a résumé of your thoughts. Make your remarks true to each child, not a generalised statement that appears on the work of the majority of the class. Use each child's name, then she knows you mean her, and not just anyone in the class.

Work in pencil so that your corrections do not dominate the poem. It is important to help the children portray more clearly the images they have in mind, but they must keep ownership of the poem. Remember that it is theirs, and must remain so.

## Presentation

Writing must have an audience, it must be read by someone.

Children must be taught to respect that audience and only offer it their best.

This chapter contains some suggestions for presenting children's work. Children should be encouraged to behave like real writers, shaping language into poetry. To call their writing poetry, at this stage, may be an exaggeration. However, it could become poetry if children know the processes involved, acquire the technical skills and are exposed to the right kind of poetry experiences.

# ACTIVITIES

## 1. Something small: 1

### Age range
Five to seven.

### Group size
Small groups or pairs.

### What you need
A small object, such as a shell, a flower, a stone, a ladybird, a piece of heather, some sand, a piece of seaweed, a small container and so on; a flipchart or large sheets of paper, a felt-tipped pen.

### What to do
Work on a carpeted area with the children seated facing you.

Give the small object to the children and ask them to pass it around, turning it over in their hands. Tell them to look at it, examining, touching and smelling it. You will find that in this way the children will start to talk about it without being asked to!

Ask for their thoughts on the object, the words and phrases that come to mind. Write the name of the chosen object on the flipchart and group the words the children say around it as they offer them. After the children have come up with the surface words like wet, cold, smooth and hard, probe for words that are at a deeper level, like brittle, fragile, crunchy, scuffed and so on.

Help the children to build up a vocabulary of words and ideas; it can take fifteen minutes or more to achieve a satisfactory list. Do not reject any word they offer initially, but once the paper is covered with their suggestions, go through them with the children to remove any that are not appropriate. This process of selecting words is an essential one for children to learn, as it plays an invaluable part in redrafting.

Some children will be able to write on their own, while the others can work with you. Together, make up phrases about the object, which you can list on a large sheet of paper. This will form the basis of the poem you will make together. Don't worry too much, at this stage, about rhythm, but ask the children what they notice about the length of the lines, the words, and how easy (or difficult) they are to say. A poem should flow, and if the lines are fairly consistent, they may have a natural rhythm of their own.

## 2. Sequencing: 1

### Age range
Five to seven.

### Group size
The whole class, then small groups or pairs.

### What you need
An overhead projector, strips of transparency, a marker pen.

### What to do
Work on sequencing helps the children to redraft their own poems. Write out each line of a well-known rhyme on a separate piece of transparency. Then place the strips on the OHP, but in the wrong order. Read the lines through with the

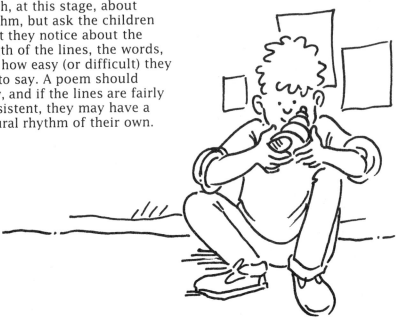

children and ask them whether they think the poem is in the right order. If not, how can they tell?

Let the children tell you how to reorder the poem. Help them to identify the rhythmic pattern and rhyming sequence as they go.

## Further activities
• Repeat this process with an unknown rhyme.
• Write out a number of rhymes, putting each line on a separate strip of card. Place each rhyme in an envelope and identify each one with a number or letter. Then you can ask the children to choose an envelope each and sort out the rhyme into what they think is the correct order.

# 3. Stimuli

### Age range
Five and upwards.

### Group size
The whole class, small groups or individuals.

### What you need
A range of stimuli – see below.

### What to do
There are lots of ways of creating stimuli to inspire poetry. The following are just a few:
• a piece of fruit;
• a favourite sweet or food;
• something small – a blade of grass, a leaf, a pine cone;
• a sound – a cry, a laugh, a scream, a squeal of brakes, a bird song, a dripping tap, running water, the wind;
• a mental snapshot or a photograph of something that caught the children's attention on a visit;
• a person, who could be a member of the family, a friend, an acquaintance about whom

they have strong feelings, or an animal;
• a feeling;
• an early childhood recollection;
• a response to the view from a window; rain, sun, snow, wind, clouds, a passer-by, a game, a vehicle.

Provide a range of poems in different styles which are relevant to your current topic, to give children an idea of the range of poetry within which they can present their ideas. Put copies of the poems up in the topic display area so that children can easily refer to them.

### Further activities
• Use first impressions and things which are visible, tangible and immediate, rather than grand themes of love, life and death.
• Read the children a poem, and then ask them to write for two minutes on the same subject but in a different style.

# 4. Observing

### Age range
Five and upwards.

### Group size
The whole class, small groups or individuals.

### What you need
An object to examine closely, magnifying glasses, photocopiable page 181.

### What to do

Help the children to learn to observe with care by drawing their attention to fine detail. Do this by asking questions similar to those below:
• What colours do you see?
• What does the shape remind you of?
• Does it make a sound?
• How does it feel to your fingers?
• Can you smell it or taste it?
• How old do you think it is? Why?
• Whose could it be?
• Where could it have come from?
• How might it be used?
• What happens when the sun shines on it, or when it gets wet, or when it moves?

Tell the children to think carefully before answering these questions. It is not a slick answer that you want, but a considered one. The children need to learn to observe in a thoughtful way.

Older pupils can use the questions on photocopiable page 181. You may also like to use it yourself, as an *aide-mémoire*, and highlight the questions that are appropriate to the current object.

## 5. Find a title

### Age group
Six and upwards.

### Group size
The whole class, then small groups.

### What you need
A number of poems copied out on to separate sheets of paper, without their titles (a complete set for each child).

### What to do
Ask the children to listen carefully to the poem you are going to read to them, because you want them to suggest a title for it after they have heard it.

Read the poem twice and discuss with them what the poem is about. What do they think would be a suitable title for it? Once the children have thought of and discussed a range of titles, tell them the actual title of the poem. Discuss the reasons why the poet's choice is different from theirs, or if it is the same, what does that imply?

Give each child the copies of the other poems and ask the class to form small groups. The groups should then select one child to read each poem while the others follow on their sheets. The groups must then decide on a title for each poem.

Towards the end of the session bring the class together and discuss the various titles each group has chosen. How do they match with the poets' choices?

Working in this way helps the children to think more deeply about the titles of poems and helps them to choose titles for their own poems.

# 6. Preparing poems for an anthology

### Age range
Six and upwards.

### Group size
Individuals.

### What you need
Poems, paper, pens, crayons, a ring-binder file.

### What to do
As soon as children can write clearly, encourage them to start making a collection of the poems they have particularly enjoyed. They can use a loose-leaf file or a book of their own making.

Don't make this a handwriting exercise, but if you stress that the poems are intended for the children's own collection, which they will be able to keep for ever, they will see the need to take special care. In this way they will become their own arbiters of quality. They can include copies of their own poems and ones written by their friends as well as copies of published poems. They should write the date, the poet's name and, if it is a published poem, the book it came from.

As the children's abilities develop, gradually introduce the calligraphic skills you use. Some children will want to keep their earlier work to show how much better they are now that they are older, but others will prefer to write out those parts of their collection again. By the end of their primary years the children will have a wealth of poetry at their fingertips and a collection to treasure.

# 7. Presentation

### Age range
Six and upwards.

### Group size
Pairs or individuals.

### What you need
A well-equipped book-making and mounting area, with a trimmer, scissors, adhesive, spreaders, needles, button thread, card, mounting paper and cartridge paper.

### What to do
Once the children have edited their work, checked spellings and ensured that their poems say what they want them to say, they can copy out their own poems as handwriting practice. If you teach yourself calligraphy, you can pass on the skill to older children. It does not take long to learn, no matter how bad your own handwriting is.

Always do your best handwriting on children's work, on the blackboard and in displays. Learn and use the school's style. Several teachers using different styles presents a confused message to the children.

Help children to make choices about presenting their work. Double-mount where possible, but put work up with steel pins so that mounts can be used several times. Use cut-out frames instead of mounts which can be placed over poems. Make the borders even. Teach children to use trimmers; even six-year-olds can learn to use them.

Children can design their own layouts and borders to present their work. Provide some borders for the children to colour in (see photocopiable pages 188 to 192) or use printed ones in colour from suppliers. The important thing is to try to match the border to the poem. The children can also use lined paper under blank sheets to help them place and space their writing and illustrations.

It is important that children share their work with each other, keep it and display it. However, not all poems need refining and presenting. Sometimes a poem is best left as it flows on to the paper.

When a poem is on a specific topic, mount it on a representative shape, for example; a raindrop,

snowflake, bubble, tree, cloud, bus, lollipop, Wellington boot, trainer and so on.

Mount poems connected with topic work amid relevant pictures and articles.

# 8. Revising and redrafting

## Age range
Seven to eleven.

## Group size
Small groups, pairs or individuals.

## What you need
No special requirements.

## What to do
The hardest skill for young writers (or older writers for that matter) to learn is self-appraisal. Children can be helped to attain this skill through class discussion of a poem, or by working together to liven up a dull poem.

Working in pairs for peer appraisal is less personal and less likely to lead to direct put-downs than working in groups, but by the end of the primary stage children should be able to work profitably together in either situation. Redrafting in groups or pairs will only be successful if children are used to this way of working on writing.

It can be helpful to put a piece of writing aside for a couple of hours or even a day or two before trying to appraise it. Coming to it fresh, children are more likely to be critical and the awkward bits will be more noticeable. Children may need to redraft a number of times before they are ready to hand over the poem.

Children should keep a file of all drafts of a poem, since

sometimes redrafting can take away the sharpness of the image, losing the poem's flow. Using the earlier drafts, these can often be recaptured. Ask the children to analyse their changes and the effect these had upon the poem.

### Further activity
Hold occasional redrafting sessions with the children. Ask them to help you redraft one of your poems, or one from a child who is stuck – provided the class works in an atmosphere of trust. Ask them to suggest the following sorts of changes:

• ways forward;
• ways to highlight the story;
• strong and weak words and lines.

This kind of experience is invaluable to children, and helps them to see redrafting as an automatic activity.

## 9. Something small: 2

### Age range
Seven and upwards.

### Group size
Small groups or pairs.

### What you need
Anything small enough to fit in the cupped palm of the hand. You can also use slides, pictures and photographs of very small things.

### What to do
Ask the children to observe the small object (see page 62) and write down their observations. They should concentrate on the fine details of the object.

They can then brainstorm for further ideas, words and phrases, making a list of the senses and exploring them in relation to the object. Using their lists, the children should try to describe the object by referring to the things that are particular to it.

While they are writing about the object the children should stay close to it so that their writing is constantly focused on it. Older children can learn to be ruthless, crossing out anything that does not pertain to the object. From the lists they can create their poem.

Give the children a time limit for writing the poem, as it will focus their minds with its sense of urgency and allow a natural rhythm, flow and logical sense to come through. Encourage the children to write quickly, without interruptions breaking their train of thought.

## Further activity

Ask the children to give you some words appropriate for an object and write five to ten of them on the board. Tell the children that they may *not* use any of these words when they create their poem about the object. This will ensure that the children seek words from a deeper level.

# 10. Sequencing: 2

### Age range
Seven and upwards.

### Group size
The whole class, then small groups or pairs.

### What you need
Paper, scissors, adhesive, an overhead projector and a transparency of the poem in its original form.

### What to do
Make copies of a short poem, preferably one with three verses. Use poems by modern poets such as Judith Nicholls, Moira Andrew, Wes Magee, Kit Wright, Michael Rosen and perhaps Spike Milligan and

choose a poem that has a recognisable sequence to it. Cut the lines of the poem into strips and reassemble the lines for each verse in the wrong order. Alternatively, type the poem on a word processor and change the order of the lines. Photocopy this new version of the poem and provide each child with a copy.

Ask the children to work in groups or pairs and try to put the poem back to its original form. You can make this a timed task if you like, to focus their thinking.

At the end of the time ask the children what clues they used to help them identify which line went where. Ask someone from each group to read out their version of the poem. Are all the versions the same? If not, why do they suppose that this is so?

Show the original poem using the OHP and ask the children to compare their versions with it. Is it the same or different? Discuss any differences and the reasons for them.

## Further activity

Ask the children to copy out a poem, but put the lines in the wrong order. They can then exchange poems with a friend and use the cut-and-paste method to return it to its original form.

# 11. Developing editing skills: 1

### Age range
Seven and upwards.

### Group size
The whole class or small groups.

### What you need
An overhead projector, a transparency, a copy of the same poem for each child.

Soft dark earth
Under the grass
One blind worm nuzzles

Lords of the air
Two crows survey the plain
Under the sky

Under the sea
Flash past in a silent stream
Three thousand tiny fish.

• portray the exact shade of meaning;
• create atmosphere;
• relay appropriate similes;
• give clear imagery:

Discuss the layout of the poem, its line length and rhythm. Examine the surface features for accuracy and consistency. They all help to clarify the meaning of the poem for the reader.

Rewrite the poem in its new form and compare it with the original.

### Further activity
Write out a poem, as prose, on an OHP transparency, and provide a copy for each child. Choose poems that have a distinct rhythm and rhyme, then move on to poems with a stronger inner rhythm but not necessarily with lines that rhyme. Work together to make the prose into a poem. Discuss with the children ways of looking for the form, whether

the poem leads easily into one particular form and where the easy or difficult bits are. Then compare your version with the original poem.

## 12. Developing editing skills: 2

### Age range
Seven and upwards.

### Group size
Pairs or individuals.

### What you need
An OHP transparency of a poem or a copy of it on a large sheet of paper, suitable pens, copies of the poem for each child.

### What to do
Type out a poem leaving out the punctuation and ignoring line breaks, and give each child a copy. Ask them to work in pairs and try to pencil in the missing punctuation. Show the children the original poem on an OHP transparency or a large piece of paper, and discuss the edited versions.

### Further activity
Write out the poem as prose for the children to work through but, this time, leave in the punctuation.

### What to do
Helping children to edit their work is vital, since without this skill their poetry writing will not make real progress. In order to gain practice children need to work on poems that are written by someone unknown. Find or write a dull poem and, with the children's help, bring it to life.

Write out the poem on a transparency and work through it with the children. Discuss the poem, the images it brings to mind and the changes that might make the poem more interesting to read. Change words so that they:
• become more vivid and descriptive;

# CHAPTER 5

# Word play

The development of language is fundamental to poetry. The following five chapters focus on language, including ways of learning more about it and exploring it through a variety of forms.

This chapter shows how, through games, children can be made to feel at ease with words and have fun with them. The activities encourage them to listen to words, to play with them and become confident in using them before they move on for a more serious look at words in Chapter 6.

# BACKGROUND

## Why bother with word games?

What we seek to do is to raise in children a love of language and an enjoyment in using it. We as teachers want children to take pleasure from seeing how others play with language and from playing with it themselves, because this enjoyment is a very important part of the craft of poetry writing.

Word games of different kinds deepen children's language skills and extend their abilities through involvement, interest and pleasure. While word games must not become an end in themselves, they do catch children's enthusiasm, and this enthusiasm can be used to develop children's experience and understanding of language.

## The advantages of word play

Word play helps children to put words on to paper. Technique can follow once this initial step has been achieved.

Techniques and form mean nothing, after all, if the content is poor, if the words are banal and the poem lacks imagery and vitality.

Word play takes many forms: from word searches to set forms; from the amusing to the ridiculous; from the spooky to the surreal. A wide range of examples can be found to suit all ages.

Nursery children will revel in simple dramatic poems like the traditional rhyme 'In a dark, dark wood'. Infants are amused by question and answer jokes, by obvious puns and 'knock, knock' jokes, by playing with words and by nonsense of all kinds. All these can often be found in traditional verses like the following:

As I was going down the
   stair
I met a man who wasn't
   there.
He wasn't there again today:
I wish that man would go
   away!

Juniors are exceedingly fond of jokes, puns, parodies, limericks and in fact, all manner of word games. Even less able readers enjoy this kind of verse or worse!

## Word games for everyone

Poor readers are not necessarily less intelligent than their more fluent classmates; they may have had such a struggle when beginning to read that the pleasure and enjoyment of reading has been lost to them. Since most of the poems suggested in this chapter are short, they are ideal to work on with hesitant or reluctant readers.

These children often gain a tremendous sense of achievement when they have mastered a whole verse or a complete poem. Initially, you may have to give them a copy of the poem to follow as they listen to you read it, but the boost that it gives them when they find they can read for fun, without too much struggle, is a joy both for them and for you as their teacher.

So long as the children understand the words that are unusual or difficult for them, then the fun takes care of itself. Make sure that you have books suitable for a wide range of reading abilities so that those with a developmental weakness in reading can also join in the fun.

As well as books of jokes and humour, it is also essential to have alongside your poetry collection a range of dictionaries for different levels of ability, as well as thesauruses, glossaries and word resources for topics, both published and home-made.

# ACTIVITIES

## 1. Anagrams

### Age range
Six and upwards.

### Group size
Small groups.

### What you need
No special requirements.

### What to do
Some names lend themselves easily to anagrams; for example, Earl = real, Kate = take, Dan = and. Ask the children to study the names of the children in their group and see if any are anagrams of other words.

The children can then look at other words and find as many anagrams as they can; for example, horse = shore, once = cone, rose = sore, roes and so on. If they are not sure whether the word they have come up with is a real word, they can always look it up in a dictionary.

### Further activities
• Can the children work out the following anagrams?

  thorn, teas, shout, stew.

• Can they create anagrams from other sayings?

## 2. Jokes

### Age range
Six and upwards.

### Group size
The whole class and individuals.

### What you need
Joke books, for example, *The Crack a Joke Book* (Puffin), *Verse and Worse* collated by Arnold Silcock (Faber and Faber).

### What to do
Many jokes are similar to free verse, with the words arranged in a specific pattern. Puns rely on using words with a double meaning. They often depend on a slight variation of spelling or sound to work.

• Some jokes duplicate the sound in the question and the answer:

  'Why did the owl 'owl?'
  'Because the woodpecker would peck her.'

• Sometimes the noun doubles as a verb:

  'Why did the cowslip?'
  'Because it saw the bulrush.'

  'Why did the lobster blush?'
  'Because it saw the salad dressing.'

*teak, race ...?*

Dr Bell fell down a well
And broke his collar-bone.
Doctors should attend the
    sick
And leave the well alone.
(Anon, eighteenth century)

Even quite young children
will have a fund of jokes like
these. Read and talk about
jokes and ask each child to
prepare one to tell to the class.

Ask the children to write up
their jokes, illustrate them if
they can and make a class joke
book.

## 3. How?

### Age range
Six and upwards.

### Group size
The whole class, then pairs or
small groups.

### What you need
An overhead projector or large
sheets of paper, felt-tipped
pens, *Not to be Taken Seriously*
by Colin West (Hutchinson).

• Jokes may depend on a word
having more than one
connotation:

'Two oranges were rolling
down a hill. One stopped.'
'Why?'
'He ran out of juice.'

• Verse appeals, whether the
humour depends on made-up
words:

There was a man called
    Michael Finnigan,
He grew whiskers on his
    chinigan,
The wind came out and blew
    them in ag'in
Poor old Michael Finnigan,
    begin ag'in.

or on double meanings:

• Sometimes a homophone
conveys the humour:

'Do you know the one about
the spider?
He spied-a juicy fly on his
web!'

• 'Knock, knock' jokes fall into
a similar category:

'Knock, knock.'
'Who's there?'
'Isabel.'
'Isabel who?'
'Is-a-bell necessary on a
bicycle?'

Handwritten on board:
How do homing pigeons find their way home?

What makes stars twinkle?

Why do cakes rise...

## 4. Acrostics

### Age range
Seven and upwards.

### Group size
Pairs or individuals.

### What you need
No special requirements.

### What to do
An acrostic is a poem in which the initial letters of each line make a word. Usually, this word also determines the content of the poem.

An acrostic is a good way of helping children to overcome the barrier sometimes caused by a blank page. It sets an exact limit on the number of lines required and is a task that can be completed at one session.

Display a number of acrostics on the poetry board for a few days before asking the children to write their own. Ask them what they notice about the poems and discuss how the words of each line tell

them on the large sheet of paper, one under the other.

Reorder the lines and rewrite any as necessary to create a poem. Try to form rhyming couplets as Colin West has done.

### Further activity
In their groups or pairs, ask the children to write down at least four questions of their own, leaving a good space between the questions. Each group or pair can then exchange their questions with another one and write the answers to the questions. These should then be returned to the originators who must try to create a poem from them.

### What to do
Read the children 'Inquisitiveness' by Colin West in *Not to be Taken Seriously*. Afterwards, discuss what the poem is about. Skip fairly lightly over the definitions, concentrating on the questions instead.

Ask the children to tell you some things they want to know about. Ten questions are quite sufficient. Write them on strips of transparency and place them on the OHP, or write the reader more about the topic of the acrostic.

Write your name, vertically, on the left side of the board. Show the class that one letter of your name will begin each line and that each line will say something about you.

Ask the children to write acrostics using their own names in the same way. The children will be able to write more easily as they are writing about themselves. They can then share their poems with the rest of the children and learn a little more about each other.

Early acrostics will tend to be rather stilted because of the imposed discipline of the form, but it does produce a more relaxed feeling about writing and a measure of success is guaranteed to all.

Once the children are familiar with the form, they can choose their own words and begin to take more care, using the best possible sentence construction – given the restrictions of the form.

## Further activities

Any noun can be used as the basis of an acrostic, so the activity lends itself to work across all disciplines.

At first, use three-lettered words like bee, bin, cow, dad, gnu, hag, ice, oil, pup. As the children become used to the format so the number of letters becomes irrelevant; it is the way language is used to explore the topic that is important.

As children become practised you can tighten up on what can be written. For example, an acrostic on the name of a character can be in the form of a character study, the one on a book title can explore the book's theme or review it, scientific acrostics can discuss an experiment or describe a creature in detail.

# 5. Chain poems

## Age range
Seven and upwards.

## Group size
The whole class and pairs.

## What you need
Poetry books that contain traditional rhymes.

## What to do
Chain writing uses the last word(s) from each line to begin the next line, for example:

Snow is great to play in,
Neville and me have
snow-fights
Outside I got hit on
the head
With a snowball - ouch!

### The Key of the Kingdom

This is the key of the kingdom:
In that kingdom lies a city;
In that city is a town;
In that town there is a street;
In that street there winds a
    lane;
In that lane there is a yard;
In that yard there is a house;
In that house there waits a
    room;
In that room an empty bed;
An on that bed a basket –
A basket of sweet flowers:
Of flowers, of flowers,
A basket of sweet flowers.
Flowers in the wicker basket
Basket on the empty bed;
Bed in the faded room;
Room in the tall house;
House in the weedy yard;
Yard in the winding lane;
Lane in the broad street;
Street in the high town;
Town in the big city;
City in the kingdom;
This is the key of the kingdom,
Of the kingdom, this is the key.

This traditional poem has a definite pattern. Each line forms a picture and that picture leads on to another, yet the successive images come together to form a composite whole – a bit like a set of Russian dolls.

Discuss this pattern with the children and ask them to suggest other subjects they could use to write a poem with a similar structure, for example, getting changed for swimming and getting dressed again.

### Further activity

Sometimes this kind of rhyme takes the form of a puzzle, as here:

> As I was going to St Ives,
> I met a man with seven
>     wives,
> Each wife had seven sacks,
> Each sack had seven cats,
> Each cat had seven kittens,
> Kittens, cats, sacks, wives,
> How many going to St Ives?

The children could write another puzzle poem beginning with the words, 'As I was...'.

# 6. Headlines: 1

### Age range
Seven and upwards.

### Group size
Pairs or small groups.

### What you need
A range of newspapers, scissors.

### What to do
Ask the children to discuss, within their groups, what a headline is, its purpose and how it is formed. If it is helpful to them, you can cut out various headlines, putting the rest of the newspaper aside.

Follow this up with a class discussion to define a headline, and then work together to devise one using the letters of your name, for example, 'Hero attacks deadly lion eating youth' (Hadley). Can they devise other ones?

The children can then work in pairs to make up headlines, using their first names and then their family names.

Give them five minutes to create as many headlines as they can and then let them share them with the class.

### Further activity
Use a range of other names to create headlines, such as the name of the school, town or village, county, places around the world or famous people.

# 7. Rules

## Age range
Seven and upwards.

## Group size
Pairs and small groups.

## What you need
Chalkboard, chalk, paper, pencils.

## What to do
Discuss the reasons for having rules. If you do not have a set for your class, ask the children for the unwritten rules they observe. List them and add to them any suggestions the children have that would help the class run more smoothly. Write out the ten most important ones and display them in a prominent place.

On another occasion ask for suggestions for making up other kinds of less serious rules, for example:
• Ten rules for eating hamburgers;
• Ten rules for curing hiccups;
• Ten rules for annoying the headteacher.

Let each group decide what they are going to make up rules about and give them ten minutes to write them down. A time limit focuses the mind wonderfully and stops children wandering too far from the task in hand. Remind them when they are half-way through their time and when there is only one minute to go.

## Further activity
Ask the children to choose something they want to avoid doing and devise ten reasons for avoiding it. Here are a few ideas:
• Reasons for not going to bed;
• Reasons for not getting up;
• Reasons for not doing your homework;
• Reasons for not going to school;
• Reasons for not going to see Great Aunt Em.

Allow the children ten minutes to do this task, and ask them to try to make their reasons unusual.

# 8. Vile verse – or worse!

## Age range
Seven and upwards.

## Group size
The whole class and small groups.

## What you need
A suitable collection of poetry books.

## What to do
Everybody remembers the rhyme 'Nobody loves me, everybody hates me, I'm going in the garden to eat worms.' Tell it to the children. How does it make them feel? What sort of sounds do they make at the end of the poem? What other words do they use when they feel revolted?

Discuss the use of alliteration – slim/slimy, fat/fuzzy – and the repetition of 'yucky' words.

Suggest that the children write a parody of this poem, beginning: 'Nobody loves me, everybody hates me...'. The poems can be as outrageous, nauseous or ridiculous as the children please!

## Further activity
Suggest that the children compose a poem about the converse situation: 'Everybody loves me, nobody hates me, I'm going...'.

# 9. Limericks

### Age range
Eight and upwards.

### Group size
Pairs or individuals.

### What you need
A selection of limericks, pencils, paper.

### What to do
Limericks, with their buoyant rhythm, make a good way to begin learning about rhythm. Part of their attraction lies in this strong rhythm and part in a combination of crudity and cleverness. Those in collections for children are generally fine, but limerick books written for adults must be read through before being put in your class library as they have a tendency to be rather explicit.

Children love writing limericks and many an attractive book has been made mixing together children's verse with adults' writing. Often it is difficult to tell the difference.

Limericks have a humour and a bouncy rhythm all their own. Count the number of beats in each line and the pattern will reveal itself. However, by reading limericks aloud children will soon get the beat and the feel of the rhythm sufficiently well to be able to write them quite easily.

From my childhood has surfaced this one which I'm sure you all know:

> There was a young lady of Ryde,
> Who ate some green apples and died.
> The apples fermented
> Inside the lamented
> And made cider inside her inside.

Here are some limericks from one of our school publications.

> There once was a boy called Mark,
> Who went to the zoo for a lark.
> But the zoo caught on fire,
> So he sat on a wire,
> Now Mark is a bright little spark.
> Louise Raymond (11)

> There once was a boy called Mike,
> Who all the girls seemed to like.
> He thought he was cool
> To act like a fool,
> Until he fell off his bike.
> Andrew West (11)

> A funny old man from Slough,
> Took all his meals with a cow.
> He said, 'It's uncanny –
> She's so like Aunt Fanny'
> But never would indicate how.
> Lucy Kitchen (10)

This is the most expensive vegetable in the world. It's made of 24 - carat gold !

## 10. Who?

### Age range
Eight and upwards.

### Group size
Pairs or individuals.

### What you need
*All the Day Through,* collected by Wes Magee (Evans), paper, pencils.

### What to do
First read to the children 'Owl' by Patricia Hubbell and 'Who's That' by James Kirkup in *All the Day Through.* The children should then pretend to be someone or something. They should choose a subject that they know a lot about and try to write what they know as succinctly as possible.

Tell the children to ask the question 'Who?' to start their poem and then answer it, using the information they have already written down, in ways that reveal more about who they are each time.

Devise a chorus stanza, either as a class or separately. Alternatively, begin each verse with 'Who's that...?'.

### Further activity
Write a similar poem, but begin with 'Someone' as in the poem of that name by Walter de la Mare.

## 11. Lies

### Age range
Eight and upwards.

### Group size
The whole class or groups of four to six.

### What you need
Strips of paper, pencils, *Rabbiting On* by Kit Wright (Collins).

### What to do
The object of this activity is to tell whopping great lies, the bigger, the more outrageously impossible, the better. Children know it is wrong to tell lies and so take great

delight in being given permission to tell them.

First read to them the poem 'Lies' by Kit Wright from his collection *Rabbiting On.* Then ask the children for a series of objects and list them underneath one another on the chalkboard. You should then call out an object from this list and ask one of the children to make up a lie about it on the spot.

Later, in groups, the children should decide what they want to lie about. It could be a carrot, gerbils, playtime, the seaside, elephants, a bucket, the moon, in fact anything. Each child in the group should contribute a lie which they write on a strip of

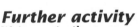

paper. For example, 'The moon is made of cream cheese'.

After sharing their 'whoppers', the children can place the strips one under the other, changing and redrafting them until the group is pleased with the result. The strips can be stuck down or rewritten for display purposes.

Make time at the end of this session to share the poems.

## 12. Beauty and the Beast

### Age range
Eight and upwards.

### Group size
The whole class.

### What you need
Pencils, paper.

### What to do
Divide the class into two teams. One team must think of and write down the most extravagant phrases to describe Beauty and the other the most dire phrases for the Beast.

Give them ten minutes for the task, and when they have finished the teams should take it in turns to read their statements; for example: 'She was so beautiful,...' and 'He was so ugly,...'.

The teams should then exchange their statements and try to 'rubbish' them. For example, if one of the statements reads 'She was so beautiful, her hair was like strands of golden silk', the other team may reply by saying 'Always getting into knots, poor love, brings tears to her eyes trying to get them out'. If another statement reads 'He was so ugly that even the alligators won't come near him', the reply may be 'At least he's still alive'.

### Further activity
Use other opposite phrases such as: 'Jack Sprat was so thin that...' and 'His wife was so fat that...'.

The phrases and answers do not have to be send-ups; they can be detailed and full of feeling, for example:

• He moved so quickly that...
He moved so slowly that...
• I felt so happy that I...
I felt to miserable that I...

## 13. Horrible humour

### Age range
Eight and upwards.

### Group size
The whole class and small groups.

### What you need
A suitable collection of poetry books.

### What to do
Read the following rhyme to the class:

Willie, with a thirst for gore,
Nailed his sister to the door,
His mother said, with
    humour quaint:
'Now, Willie dear, don't
    scratch the paint.'
(Anon.)

Ask the children what they think makes rhymes, in general, easy to remember. What is there in this particular one?

Ask them to search for more rhymes with similar attributes. They can present their collection of horrible humour in the form of a booklet to add to the class's poetry resources.

# 'I could murder a cup of tea.'

## 14. Headlines: 2

### Age range
Nine and upwards.

### Group size
The whole class, pairs or small groups.

### What you need
A range of newspapers, pencils, paper.

### What to do
Working with the class, use the alphabet and devise a series of headlines from A forward or Z backwards, for example:
• Angry buzzard caught deadly eagle for gift.
• Happy iguana jeered kindly lion.
• Merry nightingale offered paradise.
• Quiet rabbit sat tight under veranda.
• Wildebeest x-rayed young zebra.

After having worked an example through with the children, ask them to devise one in pairs or small groups. Tell the children to choose a topic for their headlines, such as animals, and stay within it.

### Further activity
Ask the children to choose a favourite magazine or paper and write alphabetic headlines for it.

## 15. The nonsense we talk

### Age range
Nine and upwards.

### Group size
The whole class and small groups.

### What you need
No special requirements.

### What to do
Our language is full of absurdities. When you think about some of the phrases we use they are quite nonsensical. Often, when we hear such phrases a quick response flicks through our minds, for example:

• 'It was so funny that he laughed his head off.' (*Who put it back on, and how?*)
• 'I should take what she says with a pinch of salt.' (*Too much salt is bad for you. How do you cope with the thirst?*)
• 'She never stops talking.' (*Not even to eat or in her sleep? How come she is still alive?*)
• 'I'm so hungry I could eat a horse.' (*Really? How? It killed the old woman, remember!*)
• 'She's getting so thin that if she isn't careful she'll slip down the plug-hole.' (*I wonder where she'll end up?*)

Ask the children to think of five similar phrases and let them devise their own responses to them.

# CHAPTER 6

# Choosing words and making them work

Ted Hughes in **Poetry in the Making** *(Faber and Faber)* writes: *'Words are tools, learned late and laboriously and easily forgotten, with which we try to give some part of our experience a more or less permanent shape outside ourselves'.*

*In poetry, the language tells the story. The meaning may be opaque, but in good poetry you can taste the words, sense the meaning, feel it inside yourself.*

*Other people's words, both spoken and written, can give us the greatest pleasure. We may appreciate the inventiveness of the way they express ideas, the careful creation of imagery or the skilful juxtaposition of words. It is the way words are used that creates the energy and the tension between the writer, the reader and the poem. All this, plus the knowledge and experience we all bring to the language, adds to the sensations we obtain from poetry.*

...in a beautiful pea-green boat...

...the golden apples of the sun...

...the thin anemones...

...in a dark, dark wood...

# BACKGROUND

As we listen or read, we each interpret the words, bringing our own context to them. Our context is determined by our own reactions to the words, the meanings we have given them and the way the words are filed and stored in our minds.

Poets struggle to match the richness of their thoughts in words, narrowing the perception gap by their choice of words on the page. There must not be one too many, or one too few; each word must count, must add to the poem.

In Chapter 5 we took a rather light-hearted look at words, having fun with them and enjoying a certain freedom. In this chapter we want to make a deliberate attempt to build up the child's storehouse of words in a more serious way.

Poetry uses words and sounds in ways that are different from everyday speech. Young children recognise this, almost instinctively, by the way they play with sounds, saying the same sound, word or phrase over and over again as they play. They repeat the jingles and rhymes that they hear and make up ones of their own. They mix sense and nonsense sounds to achieve a result pleasing to their ears and closely linked with their mood. We then lead them from this to reading, writing and enjoying poetry.

Poems for primary children should not be obstacle courses or intellectual exercises. The meaning should be easily understood from a fairly superficial reading. A poem should not be worked upon to such an extent that it is picked to its bare bones, because it is the freshness of the words and language that gives the pleasure.

When reading and writing poetry we want children to have ready access to the words they need. But how do we describe the smell of warm earth as it drinks in a summer storm or a delicate violet hiding in a hedgerow? What words describe the bubbling over with excitement when all's right with our world, or the despair when everything we touch seems to go wrong?

It's not easy, but there are ways to increase our mental storehouse of words, as well as tapping what is already there. There are ways to build up our knowledge of words; ways that work for us as well as the children.

Through peer tutoring, children can discuss ideas, imagery and word usage. Comment and criticism must be constructive, it must lead children on from where they are, pushing forward their own ideas and creativity at the same time.

Discuss a favourite poem, or a well-known one, looking at the words used and their juxtaposition, justifying their place and use. Look at their meanings, and how they are formed.

The children can keep notebooks and jot down phrases they enjoy. These jottings will make a real author's notebook, the raw material for future writing.

Our primary aim is to increase children's awareness of words, of their meaning, the sound they make, their inbuilt rhythm and pattern. The activities which follow suggest ways of working towards that aim.

# ACTIVITIES

## 1. What have we here?

**Age range**
Five to seven.

**Group size**
Pairs or individuals.

**What you need**
Large sheets of paper, felt-tipped pens, simple dictionaries, glossaries and topic word folders.

**What to do**
Write the following words down the left side of a large sheet of paper:
- size;
- shape;
- skin;
- colour;
- eyes;
- nose;
- mouth;
- feet;
- hands;
- hair;
- home;
- food;
- movement.

Use these words as prompts and ask the children to describe an imaginary being. Beside each word you can write the words and phrases they suggest. Do not accept vague words like 'big'; ask them how big the creature is, what is big about it and so on. However, the children can write 'none' against a lead word, if they so choose.

Go through the words with the children and create a poem together about this creature. Are the words the best ones that could be used? Do any need to be changed? Write out the lines and phrases underneath each other and redraft as appropriate. Check for imagery, flow and punctuation.

Once the poem has been finished the children can think of a name for their creature and draw it from the information they have given.

Put up the poem and surround it with the children's pictures.

## 2. What is it?

**Age range**
Five to seven.

**Group size**
Individuals.

**What you need**
Large sheets of paper, felt-tipped pens.

**What to do**
Ask one of the children to think of an object. She must not say what it is, but say instead what it is made of, for example, wood, flesh, material and so on. Write this word at the top of the paper.

Ask the child whether this 'something' is alive or dead and write the answer underneath. Continue asking questions to narrow down what the 'thing' might be, and list the answers the child gives. Each time an answer is given ask her if it is consistent with the information which has been given so far.

The object of the game is to give information without naming the 'thing' for as long as possible.

## 3. The rhythm of words

### Age range
Five to seven.

### Group size
The whole class.

### What you need
Large sheets of paper, felt-tipped pens, untuned percussion instruments.

### What to do
Many traditional rhymes and songs contain nonsense lines like 'Riddle-me-ree' and 'High-diddle-rum-tum-feedle' to strengthen the rhythm and to encourage audience participation. Most children know a version of the nonsense rhyme that goes something like this: 'Eeny-meaney-macker-acker-aye-dominacker...om-pom-push'.

Together with the children, make a list of words and phrases that have interesting rhythms, words that can be said out loud and made into a chant, such as 'tick-tock', 'clickety-click', 'e-le-phant', 'news-paper', or phrases like 'to and fro' and 'up and down'.

Let the children try repeating the same words or phrases in a variety of different ways until they find ones they like. They could say them over and over again lots of times or they could say them three or four times and then add another one to finish off, making a kind of rhyme or chant.

> Niggle, naggle,
> Niggle, naggle
> Pop, pop, pop.

The rhyme is not expected to make sense, that is part of the fun. The object is for children to feel the rhythm of words without the confusion of what the words mean.

### Further activity
Use the untuned percussion instruments to emphasise the rhythm of the rhymes.

## 4. Choosing the right word: 1

### Age range
Five to seven.

### Group size
The whole class or small groups.

### What you need
*Midnight Forest* by Judith Nicholls (Faber and Faber), an artefact to describe, dictionaries, glossaries, topic word folders.

### What to do
Children, like many adults, use a limited range of words. They have a familiar vocabulary within which they circulate freely. Unless opportunities are given, through reading and discussion, to widen their active vocabulary, their spoken and written structures will remain restricted.

Gather the children round you and read through twice with them the poem 'Nice Work' by Judith Nicholls in *Midnight Forest*. Discuss what

Tick - tock
Crickle - crackle
Ramshackle
Stickleback!

We like this fire engine because it is:
Colourful   Bright red   Complicated
Shiny       Fast         Interesting
Moveable                 Fun

the poem is about. Talk about some of the unusual words and what the author means when she writes 'the choice is as long as a string!'

Look at a 'nice' painting, a 'nice' model or a 'nice' new toy. What is 'nice' about it? The colour? What about the colour? Keep responding with questions to coerce the language from the children and get them really thinking. However, it is important that you do not press too hard in the beginning.

Write at the top of the sheet, 'We like this... because...' and proceed to record the words the children use to describe what they like about the subject under discussion. Have a dictionary handy and read out the definition of some of the words proffered. Does that word really say what the children mean?

## 5. What does it mean?

### Age range
Five to seven.

### Group size
The whole class or small groups.

### What you need
A large sheet of paper, a felt-tipped pen, dictionaries, thesauruses.

### What to do
Begin with a rhyme that the children all know well, for example:

Jack and Jill went up the hill
To fetch a pail of water;
Jack fell down and broke his
    crown,
And Jill came tumbling after.

Up Jack got, and home did
    trot
As fast as he could caper;
He went to bed to mend his
    head
With vinegar and brown
    paper.

Say both verses through together, and then ask the children what they think the word 'caper' means. How could they tell what the word might mean? What other words can they think of that have a similar meaning? How would it affect the rhyme if they substituted one of the other words for 'caper'?

Make a list of all the words the children come up with, and let them seek more in dictionaries and thesauruses.

Work through other rhymes, and ask the children about other specific words in the same way.

## 6. Candles

### Age range
Five to seven.

### Group size
Small groups.

### What you need
A tall fairly thin candle, an attractive wine bottle, matches, paper, pencils.

### What to do
Sit with the children round a table and place a candle, which has been stuck securely in a

wine bottle, in the middle. Discuss how candles were used before electricity, how they are made and so on.

Tell the children that you want them to watch very closely, and make a ceremony out of lighting the candle. Remind the children that they must look with their eyes and their minds, but hands must be kept away from the candle, and ensure that the children do not stare at the candle for too long.

Ask them to talk about what they see happening. If their statements are flat, ask questions like, 'What does it look like?' or 'What does it remind you of?' to encourage a more interesting response. 'Wax is dripping down the side' can become 'Dripping wax looks like icicles frozen to the candle', or 'The red wax

dribbles down the candle like tomato ketchup'.

Write the comments the children make as short statements; older infants can write the list for themselves. Cut the statements into strips and work together to organise them into a poem.

## Further activity
Display the poems with observational drawings and wax resist designs.

# 7. Questions

## Age range
Five and upwards.

## Group size
Any.

## What you need
An object or a memory for stimulus.

## What to do
Children need something specific that they can react to

when they write poetry. We need to ask the kinds of questions that provoke a thoughtful response and bring the knowledge of the experience and the words to describe it to the forefront of their minds.

With five-year-olds the outcome will be oral, or written by you; their ability to use language should not be restricted by their limited ability to write it. Older children can record their ideas in groups or pairs or by themselves, after discussion has taken place.

With experience of this way of working, children can soon begin to ask the questions themselves. To start them off, however, ask questions like the following:
• What did you think when you touched or held the object?
• What did it feel like?
• How did you feel when the thing you are describing happened?
• What did you think then?
• What do you think now?
• What did you say?
• What did another person say?
• How did you react?
• Would you like to do it again?

## Further activity
Make prompt cards for the children to refer to, aimed at a specific task.

*demanded*
*mentioned*
*explained*
*moaned*
*yelled*

*hissed*
*spluttered*
*ordered*
*uttered*
*groaned*

*muttered*
*grumbled*
*shouted*
*whispered*
*gasped*

## 8. Secret words

### Age range
Six and upwards.

### Group size
Pairs.

### What you need
Poetry or story books, paper, pencils.

### What to do
Many words have other words within them, for example, *start*. Being able to see other words within words helps children to remember them, to spell them and so to use them confidently.

Ask the children to open a poetry or story book at random and look at one poem or page to see if they can find any of these 'secret' words. Tell them to fold a piece of paper in half and on one side write the word and on the other write the other words they can find hidden in it. For example, from 'start' the children could write star, tar, art and tart. The children must not change the order of the letters to make any new words.

### Further activity
Can the children find any words that have two meanings, like 'bar' and 'can'? Or words that can be split in two, like 'carpet'? They can write these on the other side of the paper.

## 9. 100 ways to write 'said'

### Age range
Seven and upwards.

### Group size
Groups of four or six.

### What you need
Large sheets of paper, felt-tipped pens, dictionaries, thesauruses, glossaries.

### What to do
Most children will be familiar with the expression, 'If I've told you once, I've told you a hundred times...' but can they actually think of one hundred different ways of saying the same thing?

Give each group of children a sheet of paper and ask them to draw a profile of a face with an open mouth. Beyond the mouth ask them to write different words which mean the same as 'said', such as 'uttered', 'groaned', 'gasped' or 'muttered'. They should group their words in clusters of five. Ask for two examples from each group to share with the class before the groups start writing. This way each group will have a few ideas to start with. The children can use any source of words which is available to them, such as dictionaries, thesauruses, glossaries, story books and so on.

Once they have written a cluster of five words they should draw a speech bubble around them. Five is an easy number to work to and the children will be able to form clusters of five almost without counting. If they find more than one hundred, so much the better.

At another session ask the children to make a second list of the words that they found, this time putting them in alphabetical order. Make a master list by combining the lists of all the groups. Type up the master list and mount it for the children's future reference.

### Further activity
Ask the children to make a list, in the same way, of all the different words which mean 'move'.

# 10. Forbidden word list

### Age range
Seven and upwards.

### Group size
Small groups or pairs.

### What you need
A chalkboard, chalk, pencils, paper, a selection of published poems on the subject selected, thesaurus.

### What to do
Select a subject to write about, for example, ice-cream, toys or snow. Ask the children to think of words that are connected with the topic and write on the board the first half-dozen words.

Ask the groups of children to write a poem about the subject, but they must *not* use any of the words on the board. It is helpful if each group does a brainstorming session before they begin to write their poems. If the children are in difficulty they may resort to a thesaurus, but only with your permission.

After a couple of sessions the children will realise the way forbidden words are selected. Therefore, you will have to choose the words to be excluded from their current work and tell them how you chose the words.

# 11. Memories

### Age range
Seven and upwards.

### Group size
The whole class, then individuals and pairs.

### What you need
No special requirements.

### What to do
Talk with the children about the things they remember from

when they were very young. Share some of your own earliest childhood memories too.

Give the children a sheet of paper each and ask them to close their eyes. Which of their memories is the clearest? If they cannot decide, they should write the alternatives at the top of the sheet of paper (just one or two sentences will suffice). Then they can talk their memories through with a neighbour to decide which one they seem to know most about, or which they talk about most easily.

Ask the children to write their chosen memory along the long edge of the piece of paper, and then fold the paper into six to give six columns. At the top of each column they should write the name of one of the five senses, and in the last one write the words 'thoughts'.

Under each of the senses the children should list words and short phrases that describe what they can remember seeing, hearing, smelling, touching, tasting and thinking. If they can make no associations within any one column, they can leave it

blank. Tell the children to use words that really express what they saw, felt, heard and smelt.

Once they have finished making their lists, the children should use them to help with writing a poem about the memory.

When they begin to write, tell the children to focus on the most important parts of the memory; what happened, how it happened, what resulted and how they felt inside.

Once the poem is written, the children should go through it carefully, looking closely at the words and searching for the right ones, making sure that they find the exact word which will open up their memory for others to share.

# 12. Word finders

## Age range
Seven and upwards.

## Group size
Pairs or individuals.

## What you need
Dictionaries, thesauruses, glossaries.

## What to do
Children need to develop the skill of word-searching, in order to choose the word that best expresses what they want

to say, not just one that is near enough. They need to be able to pick up a dictionary or thesaurus and know how to use them to find the right word for their needs.

### Dictionaries
Provide each child with a dictionary (if possible) and ask them to open it in the middle and write down the letter it has opened at. Tell them to do this five times. Check with the children that 'M' is the usual letter.

Now ask them to open the dictionary a quarter of the way through. What letter do they find on average? Is it D? And at three-quarters do they find S?

Challenge them to see how quickly they can find particular letters. Play one half of the class against the other. Avoid having boys against girls, particularly with older primaries, so that there are fewer opportunities for sexist remarks. At first, keep to the letters which have plenty of words listed, for example, 'e' or 'w', and then gradually work through to letters which have fewer words, for example, 'n' and 'v'. Older children enjoy the challenge of 'j' or 'q' but, to be fair, let them have three attempts at finding these letters.

### Thesauruses
Show the children how to look up words in a thesaurus. Ask them to suggest a word and look it up together. Discuss the subtle differences between the various words offered and make up sentences or phrases together which illuminate these differences.

Through exploring words, children's eyes are opened to the range of possible alternatives and the need to seek words that are precisely suited to the text they are writing.

## 13. Mapping

### Age range
Seven and upwards.

### Group size
Pairs or small groups.

### What you need
Sheets of paper at least A3 size, a felt-tipped pen, poems on the chosen topic.

### What to do
Mapping is a way of setting down information. This activity is intended to focus children's minds on words they recognise but which they may not use in written work, because they do not use them in conversation.

Write the name of the topic in the centre of a large sheet of paper, and write the five senses leading out from it. Read a few poems on the chosen topic and ask the children for words that express how they see, hear, feel, smell and taste it. Write these words on the mapping chart next to the appropriate sense label.

Use the map to create a poem. For example, some delightful haikus, similes and metaphor poems were written on snowflakes and used in one of our 'Snow' displays.

• Haiku:
  Snow is falling fast.
  A great, white, growing
    blanket,
  Devouring the land.
  Alice (9)

• Simile:
  Snow is like a soft thick
    carpet,
  Snow is like a thousand mice
  Snow is like a great white cat
  Prowling round the land.
  James (9)

• Metaphor:
  Snow is a split pillow,
  Snow is falling feathers,
  Snow is a white carpet
  Covering a spinning world.
  Earl (9)

## Further activity
Use the mapping technique to explore the various aspects of a topic, whether or not you use the resulting words for a poem.

# 14. Telegrams

## Age range
Seven and upwards.

## Group size
Pairs.

## What you need
A flipchart or a large sheet of paper, felt-tipped pens.

## What to do
Write the letters of a name, one under the other, and ask the children for words that begin with the first letter. Continue until each letter has its own list of words. The children can use a dictionary or thesaurus to search for suitable words. They should then select one word from each list to create a sentence or 'telegram'.

Try out a few telegrams yourself beforehand so that you have some in reserve if the children become stuck. Not all words will create a reasonable message, so be prepared to dump words and start again.

Once the children have worked on a couple of words with you, let them work on words of their own choosing.

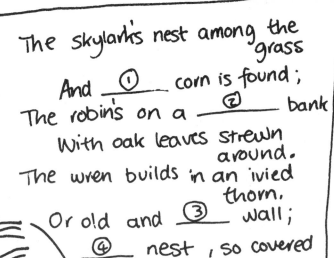

The skylark's nest among the grass
And ① corn is found;
The robin's on a ⑦ bank
With oak leaves strewn around.
The wren builds in an ivied thorn,
Or old and ③ wall;
④ nest, so covered

① blowing  ② mossy
waving       damp
shining      shady

③ ruined  ④ little
upright      mossy
dilapidated  hidden

They should check the exact meaning of the words against their needs, crossing out those that do not mean exactly what they want to say.

From the remaining words they should look for alliteration and assonance and for the word which enhances the imagery they seek to convey.

Obviously it is not necessary to do this for every word, but if you identify one or two phrases for them to work on, children will grow to be more selective, more careful in their choice of words.

one, and write it out leaving spaces in the place of some of the descriptive words. Put a number in each space and provide three or four words to choose from to fill the space (one of which must be the original word).

The children can then work in pairs to try to fill in the gaps. They should read through the poem twice before they start. Give them a time limit to complete the task.

Working with the whole class and using the OHP transparency, fill in the gaps from a consensus of opinion and then compare the result with the original poem and discuss any differences.

# 15. Choosing the right word: 2

## Age range
Eight and upwards.

## Group size
Pairs or individuals.

## What you need
A wide selection of word sources: dictionaries, thesauruses, glossaries, topic word folders.

## What to do
Tell the children to think carefully before they choose an important word. Suggest they make a list of all the words they can think of that have similar meanings, then use the word sources to locate more.

# 16. Cloze

## Age range
Eight and upwards.

## Group size
Pairs.

## What you need
An overhead projector, transparencies, paper, pencils.

## What to do
Choose a short poem, or a couple of verses from a longer

# 17. Sinister and creepy

## Age range
Eight and upwards.

## Group size
Pairs or individuals.

## What you need
Sinister, creepy and spooky poems.

## What to do
Choose a poem, such as 'The Haunted House' by Jack Prelutsky from *Nightmares: Poems to Trouble Your Sleep* (A & C Black).

Read the poem to the children and then let them join

in with it. Ask them to list the words that sound sinister to them. Even if they do not know the exact meaning of a particular word, they can judge whether it sounds friendly or threatening. What makes the difference? Can you caterwaul, for instance, in a friendly way?

After five minutes come together and discuss these words.

### Further activity
Ask the children to write a sinister or creepy poem. Make a display of their poems and decorate it with black or white shapes.

# 18. What's inside this poem?

### Age range
Nine to eleven.

### Group size
The whole class and small groups.

### What you need
A copy of 'Posting Letters' by Gregory Harrison from the collection with the same title (Oxford University Press), also in *Not 'Daffodils' Again* by Kenyon Calthrop and Janet Ede (Longman).

### What to do
There are a number of ways of exploring a poem, to help children understand it without

destroying it for them. The following questions and ideas can be used when studying the above poem.
• Read the poem at least twice. Who is frightened? Is it a boy or a girl?
• What is the child afraid of? What makes him or her frightened?
• Is the child really frightened or did he/she frighten him/herself?
• Write a movement and sound word list, taking the words from the poem.
• What is it that makes some words sound threatening? List the words and try to find what it is. Is it, for example, the long vowel sound in words like low and owl or the sibilant 's' in creep*s*, *s*idle*s*, gleam*s*, grea*s*ily? Can you think of others?
• List the descriptive words.
• Look for panic words like dash, race, blunder, fumble, leap, clang, choking and so on.
• Look for calming, comforting words and phrases like cattle stirring, soft, muzzling, familiar, old friend, home. What do they do to the poem?

• What was the most frightening thing that has ever happened to the children in your class? Is there something of which they are all afraid?
• Is fear always threatening?
• What happens to you when you feel frightened? Do you tremble, shiver, quake? Make a list of similar words.
• Do the same with words that describe feeling threatened, nervous, fearful. Compare the lists and discuss the shades of meaning that have become obvious.

### Further activity
Ask the children to write a poem about a time when they were frightened.

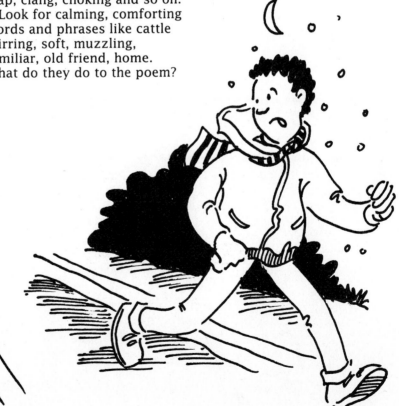

# CHAPTER 7

# Knowledge about language

Much of our language learning is absorbed by a kind of osmosis, through listening to the language in speech and in stories.

In order to have command of language and to feel at ease with it, we have to know something about it. We have to know the surface and structure of its grammar.

Virtually all the skills needed to write good English can be taught through poetry. Grammar is essential to good writing, and to teach it through poetry and games can be fun. It is more likely to be grasped this way, and is more relevant than boring, pointless exercises.

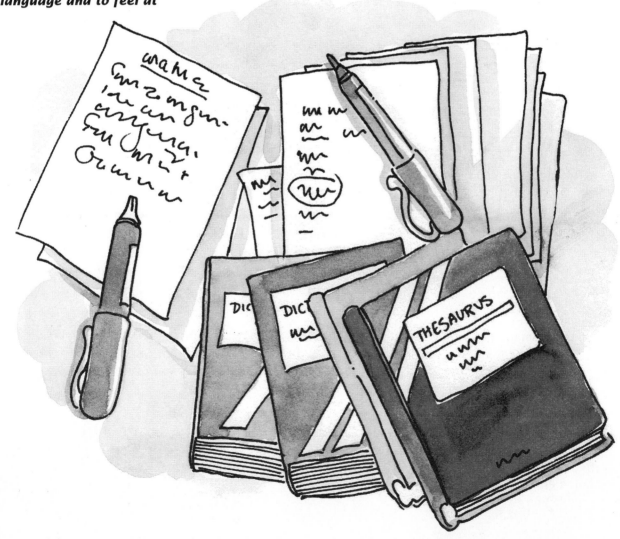

# BACKGROUND

Punctuation and spelling are not represented in speech; we may cry 'No!' but the exclamation mark is not visible. Children only learn about punctuation and spelling from seeing written language.

We know from the context whether the spoken word 'bough' refers to a tree or an inclining of the body as in 'bow', but when words are written down there are other sources of confusion. For example, we know that the written word 'bow' can also mean a way of tying a ribbon; speech, however, does not indicate the similarity of spelling.

Grammar, on the other hand, can be heard in spoken language. Some of the basic structures are with us from very early days. The small child, just beginning to speak, will say 'Want drink Mum' when she's thirsty, and she may well say 'Mum want drink?' and proffer her glass, but she will never say 'Want Mum drink' because she knows that this does not carry a message.

When she says, 'Tom hit me', she uses, without realising it, a basic sentence made of a noun phrase followed by a verb phrase. When she sings 'The mouse ran up the clock', the order is perfect; determiner, noun, verb, preposition, determiner, noun.

When children first begin to write, they simply write the way they speak, '... and then I went home and my Mum said...'. Through hearing stories and reading books they begin to learn that written language and spoken language are not the same. Later, their experience with written language tells them that there is more than one way of putting words on paper.

Words have power. Think of the power invested in the words 'light' and 'dark'. Words fascinate, delight, anger, heal and hurt, and their effect extends to the giver and the receiver alike.

We want children to know about words, to recognise their power and learn to use the best words in the best order in their poetry. Children should be made aware that the way vowels, consonants and syllables make up words can lead to the word taking on other dimensions. They can indicate movement and pace. A sense of slowness can be given by long drawn-out vowel sounds as well as by word meanings, for example, sleep, dream, flow, tired and plough.

Short vowel sounds give a more clipped and quick sense of movement, such as run, dash, skip, hop, sprint. An edge can be provided by hard 'c' or 'k' sounds, such as cold, kick, caught and so on.

This chapter takes words and looks at their place in the structure of language. It looks at ways of using poetry to learn about nouns and verbs, adjectives, alliteration, similes, syllables and synonyms amongst others. We want children to know about their language, to learn to use it clearly and economically, and to have a language with which to talk about language itself.

# ACTIVITIES

## 1. Common nouns and proper nouns

### Age range
Five to seven.

### Group size
The whole class.

### What you need
A chalkboard, chalk.

### What to do
Write a mixed list of common and proper nouns on the board. What do the children notice about some of the words? Which ones are special names? How do they know? Why are they special? What about the others? Are they special in any way?

Ask them to give you the names of everyday things. See how many they can think of in, say, five minutes. Make a list of them, and then group the nouns that are linked in some way into clusters of four, for example, 'apples, pears, bananas and grapes'. Tap the rhythm of the line and if you like it try to write other lines in a similar way.

Cluster your lines in fours or in threes with a chorus line repeated at the end of each verse.

Write up the poem and read it through with the children so that they feel its rhythm and cohesion.

### Further activity
Make a collage of proper nouns cut from newspapers, magazines, wrappers from cans, programmes, junk mail and so on.

## 2. Alliteration

### Age range
Five to nine.

### Group size
The whole class.

### What you need
A flipchart or large sheet of paper, felt-tipped pens.

### What to do
This game helps children to listen to sounds and to make links between words which, previously, may not have been apparent.

Write the word 'one' on the flipchart and ask the children to think of as many words as they can that begin with the same sound. Working together, select from these words and make up a sentence, for example, 'One wicked witch waved her wand'. Write the word 'Two' on the flipchart and proceed in the same way, for example, 'Two terrible twins took the toffee'.

Continue this process for all the numbers up to and including ten. You may have to do it in two stages with very young children, while older children could work individually or in pairs.

Once you have written all ten sentences go through the words in each one together and look up stronger, more telling words to redraft the copy, for example, 'Two terrible twins traded toffees'.

The point of this activity is to match the sound, not to maintain a constant line length, rhythm or rhyme. It doesn't matter whether it makes sense; in fact the nonsense element is part of the fun for children. Have you ever seen 'Six silly salmon singing a song'? I'll bet it forms pictures in your mind just as it will in theirs.

### Further activities
When the children start learning to play the recorder, make up rhythmic alliterative phrases to help them gain confidence in playing a note and in listening and copying

el-e-phant

before working on this kind of poetry.

Revise the work on names in Activity 8 on page 34 and then work with other words. Call a child's name and say a one-syllable word, clapping it as you say it. The child should reply by saying another one-syllable word, clapping it at the same time. Move on to words of two, three or more syllables, challenging different members of the class. Tell them to respond as quickly as they can.

Once the children have practised this a number of times they can play the same game in small groups.

## 4. Using conjunctions: 1

### Age range
Six to eight.

### Group size
Pairs.

### What you need
Pencils, paper, crayons.

### What to do
Conjunctions are words that join two ideas together. They may be there to make the writing run more smoothly or they may show a relationship between two things. With

## 3. Syllables

### Age range
Five and upwards.

### Group size
The whole class.

### What you need
No special requirements.

### What to do
Syllables give rhythm to words which you can feel (or beat) in every word that is uttered. Young children enjoy repeating and feeling the rhythm of long words even if they do not understand them. After all, what does 'Hey diddle diddle' mean?

There are a number of poetic forms that depend strictly on syllable counting, like haiku, tanka, renga and cinquains. Children need to understand and work with the syllabic rhythm of words

rhythm. We use 'Anthony Ant ate apples', 'Grumpy green grasshoppers' or 'Every elephant elevates'. Talk about what 'elevates' means and let the children enjoy the mental image of elephants being raised up and hanging in the air without visible means of support! Other ideas for alliteration include:
• using the names of each child in the group to start a line;
• using the names of towns, counties, countries, places of interest and so on.

young children it is best to start with the simple ones they know, like 'and' and 'but'.

Brainstorm together for words on a topic such as rain, toys or food. From these words ask the children to make up a list poem using the word 'but'. They should make each line the same number of syllables in length and begin the poem with a statement, followed by the conjunction, for example:

> The beach was crowded
> BUT
> we put five pies on
> a tall sand castle,
> we made a moat and
> lined it with pebbles.
> We had donkey rides and
> blueberry ice-cream....

Encourage the children to write simply, keeping the feel of rhythm in the lines. They can then illustrate their poems.

## Further activity
Using 'and' as a conjunction ask the children to write a list poem about food, for example:

> In my giant sandwich
> I had some butter
> and two pieces of meat,
> and slices of tomato,
> and....

# 5. Verbs: 1

## Age range
Six and upwards.

## Group size
The whole class, pairs or small groups.

## What you need
A chalkboard and chalk or a flipchart and felt-tipped pens.

## What to do
Explain to the children that verbs are words that tell you what is going on, and ask them to tell you as many as they can think of in two minutes.

Write the word 'sit' on the board and ask the children for other ways of saying 'sit'; for example, sits, sat, sitting. Write them on the board and ask the children to make up a sentence using one of the words. Once the children have done this do the same for 'want': wants, wanted, wanting.

## Further activity
Write the present tense of a number of verbs on separate pieces of card and put them in a bag. The children can take it in turns to pick out a card and mime the action for the class to guess. If they cannot read the words, draw little sketches to illustrate them.

# 6. Verbs: 2

## Age range
Six and upwards.

## Group size
The whole class and individuals.

## What you need
Paper, felt-tipped pens.

## What to do
Talk to the children about the things they like to do and ask them to make up a sentence about one of them. Then ask them to make up one about somebody else, perhaps a member of their family or a friend. Encourage children to express their thoughts as tightly as possible; for example, 'he sat on the bench' rather than 'He was sitting on the bench'. The first conveys the sense economically and directly. We want children to use words in this way in their writing, especially in poetry.

Make up a number of cards with phrases on them such as: 'He slipped', 'She swam', 'They sang', 'We played' and so on. The children can then take a card and illustrate it. Some children will be able to incorporate the words into their illustrations, whereas others will copy the phrase underneath and complete the sentence.

## Further activity
Write out cards with commands on them for children to illustrate, for example: 'Eat your tea!', 'Wash your face!' The words can be written in a speech bubble and the children can underline the 'doing word' or write it in a different colour.

# 7. Adjectives

## Age range
Seven and upwards.

## Group size
The whole class or small groups.

## What you need
No special requirements.

## What to do
Ask the children to close their eyes and think about a cat they know (or another creature if you prefer). After a couple of minutes, tell them to open their eyes and suggest words that describe the cats they have been thinking about.

The children can then play 'Miranda's Cat'. They must work through the alphabet choosing adjectives to describe Miranda's cat, for example:

Miranda's cat is an angry cat.
Miranda's cat is a beautiful cat.
Miranda's cat is a cuddly cat....

They could work as a class for the first few letters and then work in small groups once they have grasped the idea.

## Further activity
Divide the class in half, or into groups. Using the first letter of the alphabet the children must think of adjectives, alternating from one group to the other. See how many adjectives starting with 'a' the children can find to complete 'The Vicar's dog is an a...' or 'Granny's budgie is an a...', or any other similar phrase. When one side fails to think of another adjective a point goes to the other side and the group must think of an adjective for the next letter of the alphabet.

You do not have to go right through the alphabet in one go. Use the time you have available, but make a note of which letter you have reached and start off with this letter next time. You need not start from 'a', you could start from

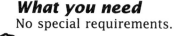

'z' or say 'Let's start at 'm' today' (or any other letter that suits your purpose).

# 8. Abstract nouns

### Age range
Seven and upwards.

### Group size
The whole class and individuals.

### What you need
A flipchart or large sheets of paper, felt-tipped pens, pencils, paper.

### What to do
Abstract nouns are names of things you cannot see, like fear, peace, happiness and so on.

Together with the children, make a list of abstract nouns. Then you can select one and ask the children to describe what it means to them. Write their responses underneath each other and, by moving lines, exchanging words, adding or cutting words, create a poem together.

Ask the children to select one of the abstract nouns themselves and write down in detail what it means to them. They can then go on to make a poem from their responses, perhaps in the way that Nicola has done:

Happiness is when I can
     swim in deep water,
It is a cool and pleasant
     feeling.
Happiness is going to school
     and doing my maths,
And getting the sums all
right.

Happiness is bouncing a ball
     and getting a hundred,
Feeling you can cuddle your
     mum.
Happiness is knowing you
     can play with the dog all
     day,
Eating yorkshire pudding.
Happiness is when I watch
     my dad shooting clays,
And getting my pocket
     money to spend on
     presents.
Nicola (8)

# 9. Similes

### Age range
Seven and upwards.

### Group size
Individuals or pairs.

### What you need
Poems based on similes, for example, 'The Fisherman's Wife' by Amy Lowell and 'Windigo' by Sylvia Mark in *A World of Poetry,* selected by Michael Rosen (Kingfisher Books); strips of paper, pencils, a large sheet of paper, felt-tipped pens.

### What to do
Read some simile poems to the children.

Tell the children that when we say that one thing is 'like' another, the description is called a simile. Ask them to think of some expressions they know which are similes. Suggest that when they make their own comparisons in poetry they try to be as imaginative and original as possible.

Take a subject such as a tomato and ask the children to describe the things it could be likened to. List them on the board or a large sheet of paper, and select from the resulting similes lines that have a similar rhythm, to create four-lined verses.

Choose another subject, give the children a strip of paper and ask them to write a simile on it. In their groups they can look carefully at the lines, redraft them as necessary and arrange the strips into an acceptable form. They can then write up the lines to make a poem.

**Further activity**
The poems can be mounted on a shape to represent the subject of the similes.

# 10. Metaphors

## Age range
Seven and upwards.

## Group size
Individuals or small groups.

## What you need
A selection of poems based on metaphors, large sheets of paper, felt-tipped pens.

## What to do
Metaphors encourage children to make mental links, by having to say that one thing *is* another, for example, 'The sun is a yellow balloon'. They also encourage the development of imagery.

Start with a subject from nature, something simple and specific like the sun, moon, stars, rain or snow. Write the word in the middle of the board and ask the children to tell you things about it, its colour, shape, what it reminds them of. Tell them to close their eyes and think what it could be turned into – with a bit of imagination – and record their responses on a large sheet of paper.

Transfer the best ones on to another sheet of paper and write them in clusters of three or four.

Snow is crunchy ice-cream,
Snow is lemonade slush
    puppy,
Snow is crushed coconut
    – Desiccated.
Maria (8)

Encourage the children to use line four to comment on the previous line, as Maria has done in this poem.

Once children have successfully completed these poems they can move on to look at topics like colour, or compare wild animals to machinery, or people to inanimate objects or animals.

## Further activity
Mount snow poems on snowflakes, sun poems on yellow paper as rays from the sun, or summer poems on petals of a flower.

# 11. Homonyms

## Age range
Seven and upwards.

## Group size
Individuals, pairs or small groups.

## What you need
*A World of Poetry*, selected by Michael Rosen (Kingfisher Books), a notebook for each child.

## What to do
Homonyms are words that have the same sound and generally the same spelling, but have different meanings.

For example, the word 'monitor' can mean:
- a senior pupil with duties to perform;
- one who listens to and reports on broadcasts;
- someone who notes the progress of a course of action;
- a receiver;
- a tropical lizard;
- a type of warship.

Explain to the children that 'homo' means 'same' and 'nym' means 'name' (actually nym is a derivative of 'onoma' which means name). The word will then have more meaning for them.

Homonyms are useful things to use when writing poems, puns and jokes that rely on this kind of word knowledge. Read to the children 'Spel it Rite' by Alan F. G. Lewis from *A World of Poetry,* selected by Michael Rosen.

Ask the children to write the heading 'Homonyms' on one of the pages in their notebooks and then fold the page in half. On the left-hand side they should then write homonyms and, on the right, list the different meanings for each word. Tell them to check the number of meanings in a good dictionary or synonym finder before writing them down.

Children are often surprised by the number of different meanings one word may have. They may know a number of them without having consciously linked them before.

### Further activity
The children can select one of the homonyms and create a short verse which depends on the homonym for its effect.

# 12. Homophones

### Age range
Seven and upwards.

### Group size
Individuals or small groups.

### What you need
A set of cards with homophones written on them.

### What to do
Homophones are words that have the same sound but are spelt differently and have different meanings, for example: ewe, yew, you; beach, beech; to, too, two.

Explain to the children that the word 'homo' means 'same' and 'phone' means 'sound' and link it with the work on homophones.

Use the set of cards to play a variety of games such as Pelmanism, dominoes, snap, matching pairs, and odd one out.

a pale pail

a bare bear

a dear deer

They should write down the poem and read it back, altering the dialogue as necessary. A question and answer poem of this sort needs short lines and implied action. The next task is to put in the punctuation, discussing between them what is required.

## *Further activity*
The poems could be prepared for presentation to the class, and some could be used in assembly or at a poetry session. Often they give rise to questions of social behaviour which can serve as a focus for class discussion.

# *13. Punctuation*

### *Age range*
Seven and upwards.

### *Group size*
Pairs or individuals.

### *What you need*
Pencils, paper.

### *What to do*
One of the advantages in using a question and answer poem, similar to the following one, is that the children have to work hard at their punctuation for the reader's sake. Without it the poem would be meaningless.

'Oi you!'
'What me?'
'Yes you!'
'Me?'
'Yeah!'
'What d'you want?'
'You!'
'What for?'
'Tell you something!'
'What?'
'Come here first.'
'Alright.... Hey!
What d'you do that for?'
''Cause I felt like it.'
'I di'n't do nothing to you!'
'No, that's your trouble.
You don't do nothing!'

Read the above poem to the children a couple of times and ask the children to discuss in pairs a possible scenario for a question and answer poem of their own. They should then create the poem by each taking a role and playing out the proposed scene, and adding a concluding statement.

# *14. Using conjunctions: 2*

### *Age range*
Eight and upwards.

### *Group size*
Pairs.

### *What you need*
Pencils, paper.

### *What to do*
Read the children the following poem which is unfinished and

ask them to work in their pairs to complete it.

Because I stayed at home
I heard the bell.
Because I heard the bell
I went to the door.
Because I went to the door....

### Further activity
Write a poem using one of the other conjunctions.

# 15. Mad meanings

### Age range
Nine to eleven.

### Group size
Pairs.

### What you need
A range of dictionaries, thesauruses, word finders, pencils, paper, crayons.

### What to do
Ask the children to make a list of words and use the sounds of the words to devise nonsensical meanings for them. Here are a few examples to go through with the children, before they start, to help them understand the nature of the task:

a primrose

• parade = help for father (pa aide);
• accord = a piece of thick string (a cord);
• grammar = the mother of one of my parents (grandma).

Later, share together the words and the mad meanings the children have devised. Make a wall display of their inventions. The children can also illustrate those that lend themselves to it.

Leave out some pieces of paper on which they can write other mad meanings as they think of them. Encourage them to keep a mad meanings page in their notebooks. These could then become a basis for a poem at a later stage.

### Further activities
Ask the children to make two words from one and write a new definition:
• father = a plump lady (fat her);

• night-time = nearly time (nigh time);
• snapshot = shoot quickly (snap shot).

The children could also draw definitions for words, for example:
• carpet = a car being kept in a dog basket, with its own food dish, being taken for a walk on a lead;
• suitcase = a suit being packed full of things for a holiday, or with the sleeves and legs tied together as handles and the middle full of clothes.

a handicap

# 16. Antonyms

### Age range
Nine and upwards.

### Group size
Pairs or individuals.

### What you need
Paper, pens.

### What to do
An antonym is a word that has contrary meaning to another one, for example antique/modern.

Ask the children to fold their paper in half lengthways, and choose an adjective to write at the top. In the left-hand column ask them to list suitable synonyms and in the right column antonyms of the word.

When one word is completed, they should rule a line across both columns and select another word to explore. For example, if you take the word 'light' you get:

- radiant;
- sunny;
- luminous;
- bright;
- glaring;
- glowing;
- lustrous;
- sparkling;
- brilliant.

The antonyms of light could be:

- dark;
- shadowy;
- shady;
- dusky;
- dim;
- dull;
- dreary;
- gloomy.

Ask the children to select a synonym from the list, with its antonym, and write a line about each one using the other words in the list to develop the meaning, for example:

Light is day, brilliant, colourful,
Dark is night, dreary, shades of grey.

### Further activity
Ask the children to take one of the synonyms and write a verse about it, then respond to the first verse by using its antonyms in the second verse.

ugly            beautiful

old      young

# CHAPTER 8

# All kinds of poetry

If children are to develop control of the medium of poetry writing in a progressive and structured way, they need to be able to experiment with new forms in a secure and supportive environment. They also need to be exposed to a wide variety of styles of poetry if they are to be able to use language effectively.

Before children can write about anything, they need to observe, discuss and examine their subject closely, and they need to have time to absorb and reflect upon what they discover. They will then be able to use this knowledge in their own writing, expressing their thoughts in forms they feel confident in using.

This chapter introduces a number of different poetry forms. Provided that poetry has been well taught in previous years, children of upper primary age will be able to use the ideas given here fairly quickly as stimuli for their own poetry writing. Middle primaries, however, will need to spend time looking at, reading and talking about the different forms of poems, reading a number of examples over several days, exploring poems written in each specific form and observing how poems of each sort are structured before they begin to write one themselves.

Younger children will need to spend even more time reading, discussing, word-hunting, exploring, finding, examining, comparing, observing, drawing and making, before they can express their thoughts on a subject through writing. They will struggle to get words down, and will need the freedom to do so (or the help of an adult scribe) before having the added restrictions of form imposed on them.

# BACKGROUND

## *Forms and styles*

Children use other writers' forms and styles as a way into poetry because they provide them with a format to work within. Not all children enjoy the freedom that unrestricted choice gives them. Given a form, they know they can achieve something, and provided the finished piece contains the tiniest scrap of their own ideas, it will have been worth while. Brief, structured, concentrated forms, like haiku, are popular because the children know the parameters they have to work within. They are not working in a void, the beginnings are established.

Brainstorming encourages children to be adventurous, to plunder their imaginative worlds for words which they can then use precisely and exactly on the page in their chosen form. Once their thoughts are down, the form of the piece can be honed into shape. 'The rain was pouring from the gutters' can become 'Rain poured from the gutters', or 'Gutters poured with rain', or 'Rain cascaded off the gutters'. The form and rhythm the writer has in mind will each dictate the way a piece is edited.

This chapter looks at poetic forms and at ways of putting words down using definite controls. By fitting their ideas, thoughts and words into the forms of old rhymes and poems by contemporary writers, the children will become more confident and mature writers themselves.

# ACTIVITIES

## 1. Pattern poems: days and months

### Age range
Five to seven when used as a class activity; eight and upwards when working individually or in small groups.

### Group size
The whole class, small groups, pairs or individuals.

### What you need
A collection of pattern poems for the days of the week and months of the year.

### What to do
Many poems and rhymes about the days of the week and the months of the year follow a very similar pattern; they take the form of a list of the days or months, mentioning the attributes of each. The best known rhyme of this sort is probably 'Monday's child'. Two other traditional rhymes which follow the same pattern are 'Solomon Grundy' and 'Sneeze on Monday, sneeze for danger'.

The following rhymes and poems also keep to the same form:

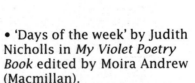

• 'Days of the week' by Judith Nicholls in *My Violet Poetry Book* edited by Moira Andrew (Macmillan).
• 'The Garden Year' by Sara Coleridge in *The Oxford Treasury of Children's Poems* edited by M. Harrison and C. Stuart-Clark (Oxford University Press).
• 'When I Was One' by A.A. Milne in *Now We Are Six* (Methuen).

Read, discuss and display a range of poems and traditional rhymes that conform to the same pattern. Ask the children to identify what they have in common.

Younger children could then work together to choose days or months to start each line of a poem, and build a rhyme following a pattern similar to one of these poems.

Older children can select from themes like food, hobbies, books, flowers, animals or even the daily timetable to make their own 'days of the week' pattern poems. They should choose one theme and relate aspects of it to each day. Having listed what they may do on each day, they can work with the words and phrases to turn them into a poem.

### Further activity
The children can search for other similar pattern poems and make an anthology.

## 2. Pattern poems: numbers

### Age range
Five to seven when used as a class activity; eight and upwards when working individually or in small groups.

### Group size
The whole class, small groups, pairs or individuals.

### What you need
A collection of pattern poems.

### What to do
Read examples of number rhymes and ask the children to identify the pattern. Use rhymes that count up to ten and back down to zero, for example:
- 'One, two, buckle my shoe...';
- 'One, two, three, four,
  Mary at the cottage door...';
- 'One, two, three, four, five,
  Once I caught a fish alive...';
- 'One little green elf lived in a tree,
  Two little brown owls kept him company...';
- 'Five currant buns in the baker's shop,
  Big and round with sugar on the top...';
- 'Five fat sausages,
  Sizzling in the pan...';
- 'Five little rabbits
  Sitting by the door...';
- 'Ten green bottles...'.
  You could also use various rhymes made up for counting cherry stones or sneezes, for example:
- 'One for sorrow,
  Two for joy...';
- 'Tinker, tailor, soldier, sailor...';
- 'One I love, two I love, three I love I say,
  Four I love with all my heart...';
- 'Once a wish, twice a kiss...'.
  The children can then make up a number rhyme either for cherry stones, sneezes or counting up to ten and back. Older children can create rhymes for younger children to use as counting games.

## 3. Narrative poems

### Age range
Five to seven when used as a class activity; eight and upwards when working in pairs or groups.

### Group size
The whole class, small groups or pairs.

### What you need
A collection of narrative poems, large sheets of paper, thick felt-tipped pens.

### What to do
Narrative poetry permeates our literary heritage in verse,

Everyone was looking forward to the outing.

We all had a lovely time but Jenny and Neema got lost in the maze!

Finally they managed to get out just in time!

ballad and song; from 'The Hairy Toe' (Traditional American) and 'The Wraggle Taggle Gypsies' (English ballad), to 'Widdecombe Fair' (Devonshire folk song) and 'The Lambton Worm' (Northumberland folk song). The tradition includes Chaucer's 'Canterbury Tales', 'Beowulf', 'The Rime of the Ancient Mariner' (Samuel Taylor Coleridge), 'Goblin Market' (Christina Rossetti) and 'The Highwayman' (Alfred Noyes), as well as more contemporary works by poets such as Charles Causley.

Narrative poems can be used to lead children from the light-hearted rhymes and comic verse of childhood into the deeper realms of more serious poetry. They give children a chance to sample not only some good stories, but also a range of compelling rhythms and regular verse and a fund of evocative language. The narrative form has pace and verve, weaving its own kind of spell.

Stories are an essential element of listening, reading and writing and this includes stories written in verse. These are often more rapidly told than stories written in prose, building one picture upon another so that interest is retained, even for the youngest or least able child.

Read narrative verse to the children which is suited to their age and maturity and then let them tell you the story of the rhyme.

Use stories with a chorus such as 'The Gingerbread Man', and work together to try and turn the story into a rhyme, repeating the chorus between each verse.

When the children write in this form for the first time, as with any new form, work together from the board or flipchart. With the younger children work together until they have sufficient control over their writing to work in pairs or small groups.

If you are not adapting a traditional tale into verse, you need to decide what the story is going to be about. It may be something that has happened to one of the children, it may be an anecdote or something you have done together. Discuss with the children the idea of the beginning, middle and end of a story and draw three boxes on the paper. Draw or write in the first box a phrase to say what happened first in the story. Do the same in the second box for the middle part of the story and the third box for the end of the story.

Draw in the spaces between the boxes the other things that happened in the story. This will leave you with a story told in five pictures. As the children learn this way of working they can increase the number of boxes to seven, or dispense with them altogether.

Ask the children to look at each picture and talk about what is happening in each one. Write a short sentence or two for each picture and use these sentences to create a rhyming couplet or a four-lined verse.

Keep the rhythm consistent and redraft the lines as necessary. Look at the quality of the words used. Are they the best or most suitable ones?

Write out the poem on a large sheet of paper so it can be seen as a whole, and edit it as necessary.

# 4. Chorus line

### Age range
Six to eight in teacher-led groups; nine and upwards otherwise.

### Group size
Individuals, pairs or small groups.

### What you need
A selection of anthologies which contain poems with different kinds of chorus line.

### What to do
Read to the children a number of nursery rhymes and poems that depend on repetition in the form of a chorus line. Encourage them to say what they think the connection is

between the poems and to think of other rhymes they may know which have chorus lines or phrases, for example:
• 'Here we go round the mulberry bush';
• 'London Bridge is falling down';
• 'The Owl', where 'Wisky, wasky, weedle' (line 2) and 'Fiddle, faddle, feedle' (line 4) are repeated in each verse;
• 'Lavender's blue' where 'diddle, diddle' is repeated;
• 'A farmer went trotting upon his grey mare,
  Bumpety, bumpety bump!...';
• 'Soldier, soldier will you marry me,
  With your musket, fife and drum?'
  'Oh no, sweet maid, I cannot marry you,
  For I have no (coat) to put on.'
  So off she went to her grandfather's chest
  As fast as she could run,
  And brought him a (coat) of the very, very best,
  And the soldier put it on.'

Older children will appreciate the lyric quality of the two-verse chorus element in the question-and-answer poem 'Dream of the Fair Forest' by Judith Nicholls in *Magic Mirror (Faber and Faber)*.

Read 'When the Wind Blows' by John Foster in *My Violet Poetry Book* edited by Moira Andrew (Macmillan). Tell the children to look at:
• the way the chorus line begins each couplet;
• the rhymes that end each couplet;
• the verbs that convey both sound and movement;
• the telling vowels – short in 'flap' and 'slam', long in 'groan' and 'creak';
• the sibilant sounds in 'swish', and so on.

Look also at Wes Magee's 'Calling, calling' in *Dragon's Smoke* (Basil Blackwell), a well-crafted poem with clear, vivid images in three short verses.

Ask each group to search through anthologies for chorus poems and to make a display of the ones they like best on an A1 sheet of paper. Remind them that handwriting, presentation and layout are just as important as the way a poem is illustrated!

## Further activities

• Ask groups of children to prepare one or two poems that they enjoy and perform them to the rest of the class.
• Ask the children to make an anthology of chorus line poems.
• Ask each child to write a chorus line poem. One successful way to start is to use a four-line verse form with the last line becoming the chorus. The children can write down the outline of an incident or event using the names of

the people involved as the chorus line, for example:

> In August nineteen-eighty-
> five
> We stayed with Great Aunt
> Bea;
> Mum and Dad were there
> with us –
> Pat, and Val, and me.

The scene is then set to unfold the story of what happens to 'Pat, and Val, and me'. With the pattern of the first verse established, and the story line clear, the children will be able to get into the swing of the rhythm. They will probably find that the rest follows surprisingly easily.

# 5. Shape poems: line length

## Age range

Six to eight when used as a whole-class activity; nine and upwards when working individually or in pairs.

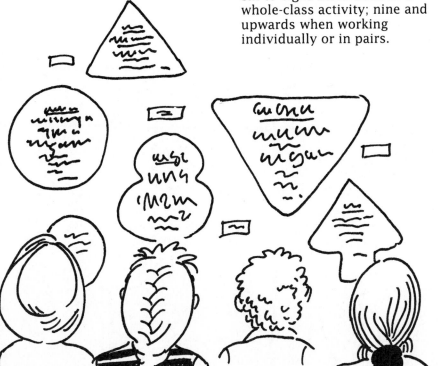

## Group size

The whole class, pairs or individuals.

## What you need

A collection of shape poems.

## What to do

Display examples of shape poems in the classroom and ask the children to identify the different types of pattern.

Different patterns can be made by altering the number of words or syllables used in each line. For example:

> I steady the heavy rifle,
> Square up the sights,
> Tighten the trigger,
> Bunny rabbit
> Zapped.

This poem only uses fifteen words. Line one introduces and sets the scene, and line five provides a one-word climax. Usually, as in the above example, the form used is five, four, three, two, one, but the numbers can also be in reverse.

If using the number of syllables to create a pattern, the usual sequence is two, four, six, eight, two as in 'A Question of Plague' by Judith Nicholls in *Magic Mirror* (Faber and Faber). This writer also uses a less common variation, two, three, four, five, eight, in her poem 'Please Pharoah'.

Ask the children to choose a personal event which was dramatic or memorable and make a list of associated words

or phrases. They can then create their own pattern poems.

### Further activity
Look at other forms of pattern poems, for example the hourglass shape using five, four, three, two, one, two, three, four, five words per line.

## 6. Copy a poem

### Age range
Seven and upwards.

### Group size
Pairs or small groups.

### What you need
A poem that provides a good example of a certain poetic form, a copy of the poem for each child or one large copy that everyone can see.

### What to do
You may find it helpful to look at and work through with the children the activities 'Substitution' and 'Active Listening' on page 35 in Chapter 2, before working on this activity.

Display and read to the children poems that lend themselves to imitation. The following are just a few suggestions, but your collection of poetry books will be full of other suitable ones:
• 'The Toaster' by William Jay Smith in *All the Day Through*, a collection by Wes Magee (Evans).
• 'My Puppy' by Aileen Fisher in *All the Day Through*.
• 'Four Little Tigers' by Frank Jacobs in *A World of Poetry*, selected by Michael Rosen (Kingfisher Books).
• 'The Long-sought-after Proof that Money Grows on Trees' by Louis Phillips in *A World of Poetry*.
• 'Gone, Gone, Gone' by Anne English in *My Red Poetry Book*, edited by Moira Andrew (Macmillan).
• 'Movements' by Maggie Holmes in *My Red Poetry Book*.

Talk with the children about the content of the poems and discuss how the poet handles the subject.

Ask them to link the rhyming words, and identify the pattern of the rhyme or the chorus lines. Underline the words carrying the strong beats on each line.

Ask the children to write their own poems using the same rhyme and rhythmic pattern, but not the same subject. (With younger children, write one together.)

Through copying different poetic styles the children will gain practice in a range of technical skills associated with writing poetry.

## 7. Mini mini-poems: 1

### Age range
Seven and upwards.

### Group size
Pairs.

### What you need
No special requirements.

### What to do
Mini mini-poems are usually confined to one idea or concept. The subject of the poem forms the title and two or three lines of text explore it. The lines usually rhyme, as in this poem:

> *Aeroplane*
> I
> Fly
> High
> Barry Hunt (7)

Ask the children to make a collection of the smallest poems they can find, with less than ten words for preference.

When the children begin to write their own mini mini-poems, once they have decided what they want to write about, they can use a number of techniques to refine their ideas and find the precise words they need.

Mapping can be used to explore a topic or subject. The children should write the topic in the middle of a sheet of paper and write any words or ideas that come to mind around it. They can then draw lines between connecting or contrasting ideas, and use a synonym-finder or word file to add further words and make other links. They can then search for words on the word-map which have the same rhythm, similar ideas, assonance and alliteration, and

list these so they can begin working on their poem.

Redrafting is an essential feature of these very short poems to maximise the meaning brought by each word.

### Further activity
If the subject of their poem is suitable, the children can draw it and make their poem part of the drawing. Barry drew an aeroplane and tied a flag to the tail on which he wrote his poem.

# 8. Links in a chain

### Age range
Seven and upwards.

### Group size
Pairs.

### What you need
A variety of chain poems.

### What to do
These poems are similar to the chain poems in Chapter 5 (see page 77), but they are narrative poems in which each link has a verse to itself. Their rhythmic

pattern makes them ideal to be used as songs.

The form used in the skipping rhyme below is rhyming couplets, with the second subject of each verse becoming the first subject of the next:

Nebuchadnezzar, King of the *Jews*
Bought his wife a pair of *shoes*.

When the *shoes* began to *break*,
Nebuchadnezzar bought a *snake*.

When the *snake* began to *sting*,
Nebuchadnezzar bought a *ring*.

When the *ring* began to *rust*,
Nebuchadnezzar turned to *dust*.

Another example is 'Hush little baby, don't say a word, Papa's going to buy you a mocking bird'.

A statement or question and the response to it can also form a linking theme, as in the song, 'There's a hole in my bucket, dear Liza, dear Liza'. In this form a question is asked in one verse and answered in the next. The answer gives rise to another question which becomes the third verse, and so on. It is cyclic in that the last verse and the first are virtually the same: 'But, there's a hole in my bucket...'.

To write these poems, tell the children to fold their paper

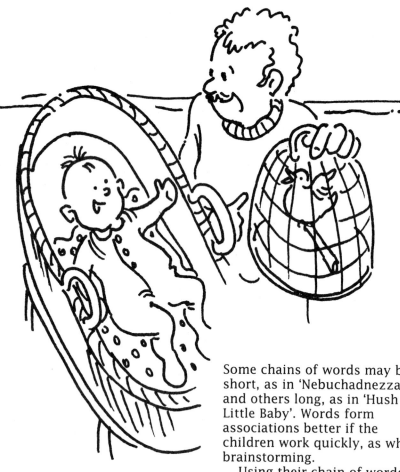

in half lengthways and write a noun on the left half of the paper and associated verbs on the right. When they have listed several verbs they should draw a rule across the page under the lists. They should then write a list of nouns that rhyme and are associated with the previous list of verbs. Again when they have finished they should rule another line. This way the children will build up groups of words from which they can select for their poem. After four groups have been completed, they can start to create the poem.

If the children get stuck, tell them to rule two lines across the page and start a new chain.

Some chains of words may be short, as in 'Nebuchadnezzar' and others long, as in 'Hush Little Baby'. Words form associations better if the children work quickly, as when brainstorming.

Using their chain of words, the children can build the structure of the poem. It can be original or it can follow the form of an existing poem. They will see the way the words are running, which will dictate the text which holds the poem together.

By moving the lines around and changing words, as necessary, the poem grows. It doesn't always work, of course, but the same can be said of any other poetic form.

## Further activity
Redraft and edit the poems as necessary. Mount and display them on the poetry board along with published or well-known examples of the same form. Alternatively, make a booklet of the children's poems.

## 9. Kennings

### Age range
Eight and upwards.

### Group size
Small groups or pairs.

### What you need
*Poems for 7 Year Olds and Under* chosen by Helen Nicoll (Puffin), *Magic Mirror* by Judith Nicholls (Faber and Faber).

### What to do
Kennings are words or groups of words we use to describe something without using its correct name. Originally they came from Anglo Saxon and Old Norse poetry, and consisted of compound metaphors such as 'oar-steed' for 'ship' or 'bone-house' for 'body'. In a more flexible way, kennings can also be used in modern poetry. They are more than synonyms; they highlight what a thing is like, or an action it can take, for example:
• lookers – eyes;
• smeller – nose;
• champers – teeth;
• snuggle-down – bedtime;
• goggle-box – television;
• fact-finder – encyclopaedia.

Read the children the poem 'Four stiff standers' in *Poems for 7 Year Olds and Under* chosen by Helen Nicoll, and ask them to interpret it and discover what it means.

Show the children the poem 'Frogspawn' by Judith Nicholls

in *Magic Mirror*. This is a visual poem that uses a list of kennings to describe the stages of growth from spawn to frog. Words for tadpole such as 'madtail' and 'miniwhale' are so apposite!

The children should then select a topic and make a list of words that describe the subject or what it can do. These kennings can then be used to write the poem.

Another way to do this is to write about the progression of time, for example the seasons, the day, the stages of life, a journey, the life cycle of a butterfly and so on. Make up a kenning for each stage of the sequence and use this for the basis of a poem.

Poems of this type are generally made from one- or two-word lines in two- or four-line stanzas. Therefore, once the children have listed their kennings in order, very few other words will be needed to complete the poem.

## Further activity
Look at the way Judith Nicholls has presented her poem and suggest to the children that they individualise theirs in a style appropriate to their subject.

# 10. Mini-poems

### Age range
Eight and upwards.

### Group size
Pairs.

### What you need
A display of mini-poems, including 'Bird-noise' by Geoffrey Summerfield in *Dragon's Smoke*, collected by Wes Magee (Blackwell), 'Tiger' and 'Wolf' in *Midnight Forest* by Judith Nicholls (Faber and Faber), 'Spill' and 'Clockface' by Judith Thurman in *A Fourth Poetry Book*, compiled by John Foster (Oxford University Press).

### What to do
Mini-poems usually contain two or three words per line, in a four-line verse. The use of language has to be precise and exact. The words should encourage the reader to read slowly, several times, and reflect upon the imagery created.

Discuss the descriptive language in 'Bird-noise' by Geoffrey Summerfield in *Dragon's Smoke*, the imagery in 'Tiger' and 'Wolf' by Judith Nicholls in *Midnight Forest*, and the depth of meaning in the two poems by Judith Thurman in *A Fourth Poetry Book*.

By searching through anthologies, each group can build a collection of mini-poems. After making a small book, about 10cm × 15cm, the

children can write a poem on each page and illustrate it with small, carefully observed, detailed drawings. They could also copy the poem out so that it can be displayed and then write underneath it why they like the poem, or tell the class why they like it.

After the children have completed work like this, when they come to write their own mini-poems they will be well prepared for the form. They will know how to cut out words they do not need, removing extravagant language and unnecessary adjectives. They know that each word has to earn its place if the mini-poem is to encapsulate the moment, the mood or the image.

## 11. Mini mini-poems: 2

### Age range
Eight and upwards.

### Group size
Pairs.

### What you need
A4 paper.

### What to do
Mini mini-poems can deal with contrasting ideas, for example:

> *Childhood memories*
> Glowing, golden light,
> Spooky, bat-black night.

When writing about contrasting themes, ask the children to take a sheet of A4 paper and fold it in half. They should head each column with one of the themes they intend to contrast, for example themes like summer/winter, hot/cold, noise/silence. In their pairs, let them brainstorm the words for each theme.

When they have compiled lists for each theme, thought about them and added to them, the children should search their lists for words of the same rhythm or assonance, and which convey similar ideas. They can use these words to begin working on their poems.

Redrafting is an essential feature of these poems to ensure that the exact image the writer seeks is portrayed.

### Further activity
Children who have worked on contrasting themes can write them as positives and negatives, white on black and black on white, or use opposite colours like red and green, orange and blue.

## 12. Ballads

### Age range
Eight and upwards.

### Group size
The whole class.

### What you need
A selection of ballads suited to the age group.

### What to do
The oral origin of ballads means that they depend on strong rhythm and metre, simple, regular rhyme, repeated words and choruses and clear details of events and characters. They are easily remembered, yet draw both the teller and the listener back again and again.

The most common form of ballad is a four-lined verse

rhyming at the end of the second and fourth lines:

> 'Twas in the merry month of May,
> When green buds all were swelling,
> Sweet William on his death bed lay
> For love of Barbara Allen.
> (British, seventeenth century)

Another common form is a four-lined verse made from two rhyming couplets, for example 'Casey Jones' taken from *A World of Poetry*, selected by Michael Rosen (Kingfisher):

> Come all you rounders, I want you to hear
> The story of a brave engineer;
> Casey Jones was the rounder's name,
> On a big eight wheeler of a mighty fame.

The third common form is again four-lined but with the first three lines rhyming and the fourth based on a repeated theme. This particular traditional British ballad (remembered from my childhood) is a good one to use with younger children:

> Fox went out on a chilly night,
> He begged for the moon to give him light
> For he'd many miles to go that night
> Before he reached his den O!
>
> First he came to a farmer's yard,
> The ducks and the geese declared it hard
> That their nerves be shaken and their rest so marred,
> By the visit of Mister Fox O!'

Another version of this ballad can be found in *Poems for 7 Year Olds and Under* chosen by Helen Nicoll (Puffin).

Read a ballad to the children two or three times and suggest that they close their eyes while listening. Afterwards, ask them to tell the story of the poem, to talk about the images it forms in their minds and the kind of feelings they have about the poem. Encourage them to use lines from the poem they like, or which explain what they want to say.

Children can search through anthologies for examples of old and modern ballads, as well as writing their own. It is best for them to start writing short ballads of three or four verses before moving on to longer ones.

A long ballad is best written as a group poem. Together, the children should decide on a subject for the ballad, work out the rhyming pattern they intend to use and then work in pairs to complete different sections. When they link the sections together it is important that the story

follows through smoothly. Finally, they can work together to redraft and edit the ballad.

A word processor is a good means of transferring a joint poem to print.

### Further activity
Make a book of ballads, illustrated by the children.

## 13. Haiku

### Age range
Eight and upwards.

### Group size
Individuals or pairs.

### What you need
A selection of haiku poems, paper, pencils.

## What to do

Haiku are miniature poems, snapshots, sharp, clear and perceptive.

A haiku consists of 17 syllables in three lines of five, then seven, then five syllables, written in the present tense. This form was laid down by Matsuo Basho (1644–1694) to be an objective description of nature suggesting one of the four seasons. A haiku depicts a moment or a feeling, linking it with comments on the essence of the subject or drawing upon the particular example to generalise about life itself. Haiku evokes a definite emotional response, capturing a glimpse of an elemental truth.

Nowadays the subject-matter of haiku is treated less strictly and they can be deeply intellectual as well as intuitive. In essence the true form remains, that is, the art of expressing much in a few words while implying or suggesting more.

The first line of a haiku should discuss the thing itself, setting the scene. The second line should describe it or focus on an element of it. The third line should be a summing up or a telling comment on what the previous lines express *in toto*. A haiku is therefore rounded, a complete entity in itself.

There are so few words used in a haiku that each one has to be exactly right. The words have to be moved, exchanged and reorganised in a way that prose writing never asks of the writer. A haiku may use alliterative initial, medial and final sounds, with carefully-chosen consonant and vowel sounds affecting pace and mood. Haiku are brief, and this very brevity aids children who have difficulty in writing at length.

Read a range of haiku to the children. Take your time over them, talking about what each line expresses so that pupils come to understand the form. Some haiku will vary from the five, seven, five syllabic form because of the effect of translation from Japanese into English.

Make up one or two haiku together. Ask the children for suggestions for a topic for line one, preferably something to do with nature, and then work out a five-syllable line together. Ask for descriptive phrases for line two, and write them on the board. Select the best two or three and cut out any unnecessary words, changing other words around until you have an effective middle line. Together, you can work out a powerful last line.

Another way of working is to brainstorm a given topic, perhaps something you can see or touch. First, get the children's ideas down, and then you can help them to trim the poem to the appropriate shape, size and form. The first and second lines generally come without too much trouble; it is the last line that often takes the time.

The following are some examples of children's haiku:

It's really snowing,
I'm bursting with excitement
To build a snowman.
Jon (8)

Freezing white crystals
Of snow, falling on my hand
Dissolve straight away.
Simon (8)

## Further activity

Use music to represent haiku, and explore the sounds suggested by the poems. The children can compose pieces of music for their haiku. The music can set the scene for the haiku and conclude it, or serve as an accompaniment. The music need not beat the pulse, it can be used for emphasis or mood.

# 14. Tanka

## Age range
Eight and upwards.

## Group size
Individuals and pairs.

## What you need
A selection of tanka poems, paper, pencils.

## What to do
A tanka is similar to a haiku, but has 31 syllables arranged in five lines in the form five, seven, five, seven, seven, almost like two verses. The last two lines should provide a contrast to, or comment, on the first three; for example, the first three might describe a storm and the last two the aftermath or the peace that follows.

Work on haiku prepares children for writing tanka. Like other syllabic forms they require children to be selective in their choice of words, saying as much as they can in as few words as possible. They also encourage children to think deeply about one idea and present it in such a way that it becomes vivid to the reader.

Read some tanka poems to the children. Talk about them in depth, and then write one or two together. This should enable them to get started.

## Further activity
In the oldest Japanese anthology, the *Manyoshu*, there is a song in tanka form written by two people. Later this practice became quite common. Let the children pair up and each write the beginning three lines, then exchange poems and add the two remaining lines as a response.

# 15. Cinquains

## Age range
Eight and upwards.

## Group size
Pairs.

## What you need
An object to brainstorm, paper, pencils.

## What to do
Cinquains are short poems, generally syllabic, which fit the rhythms of the English language rather better than the Japanese haiku or tanka forms. These poems have 22 syllables in lines of two, four, six, eight and two syllables. The tightness of the measure forces children to be selective in their choice of words so that the meaning is conveyed crisply and clearly.

Create a word store by looking at a chosen object. What can the children see, hear, smell and feel about it? Go through the list and cross to mind. The words the children use to write their poems need not come from the word store; it is only there to focus their thinking and to bring responses to the forefront of their mind.

When children first write cinquains the lines can be allowed to run on, giving the poem smoothness and continuity, but the last line must have impact.

As children become more experienced they can be introduced to a more disciplined form:
• line one: title;
• line two: describes the title;
• line three: an action of some sort;
• line four: a feeling about the title;
• line five: a synonym of the title.

When the poem is written, the children should say it over and over again in their heads or softly out loud, listening to

the tune of the poem. If something doesn't fit or sounds awkward, they can change it until it feels right. Remind them to keep the original so that the essence is not lost in the redrafting and editing.

### Further activity

The children can try the same activity with patterns of one, two, three, four and one words per line. The children have to think very carefully about the words they choose so that an inner rhythm holds the poem together.

# 16. Four-lined verses

### Age range
Nine and upwards.

### Group size
Individuals or pairs.

### What you need
A stimulus, for example, a photograph, a picture, an object or something connected with a current topic.

### What to do
This activity can be used to introduce children to one way of copying the form of a poem. The activity is specifically tailored to the poem which follows, but it can of course be adapted for other poems.

Read through the poem below with the children.

Look at the winter squirrel;
Nimble, nose-twitching, nut-seeker, diviner,
Finding hidden caches of nuts,
Bright-eyed, bushy-tailed, stomach-filled, satisfied.

Show the children the stimulus you want them to use for the poem. Using brainstorming techniques, the children should make lists of words connected with the stimulus. To do this they need to fold a sheet of paper into four lengthways. In the first column they should write adjectives connected with the stimulus; in the second, hyphenated words ending in 'ing' (nose-twitching); in the third, hyphenated words ending in 'en' or 'ed' (bright-eyed) and in the fourth hyphenated words ending in 'er' (nut-seeker).

When the lists are completed the children can write the poem using the following format:
• line one: Look at...;
• line two: Four words from

the lists that go together well.
• line three: The subject does something;
• line four: Four more words that explore or support line three.

Work through one or two examples with the children before letting them work by themselves.

# 17. Playing with the form of a poem

### Age range
Nine and upwards.

### Group size
Pairs.

### What you need
A large sheet of paper, felt-tipped pens, a short published poem written out as prose in sentence form.

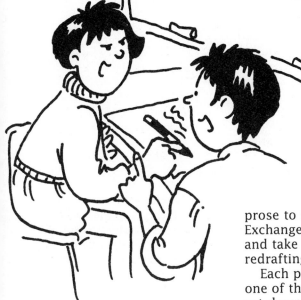

*The queen she sits upon the strand, fair as a lily, white as wand: seven billows on the sea, horses riding just and free, and bells beyond the sand.*

### What to do

One of the things about writing a poem is that once you have put down what you want to say you can alter the form until you find the one that seems right for the poem.

A poem does not have to have rhyming lines, but it must have an inner rhythm, its punctuation combining with line breaks to emphasise what the poem is saying. The lines can be long or short, grouped in a set arrangement or broken up as the poem demands.

Use a short published poem that you have written out as prose, or a short paragraph you have written yourself. Experiment with the children with ways of laying out the prose to make a poem. Exchange words, add new ones and take away existing ones, redrafting as necessary.

Each pair can then choose one of the following ideas to set down the poem. Make sure that every form is covered.
• Make each line two, four or five words in length.
• Start with a one-word line, then two, and so on.
• Go from line lengths of one to four words and back to one again.
• Write a cinquain, a haiku or a tanka (see pages 123 to 125).
• Split the paragraph into two or three ideas or aspects to make verses.
• Write the poem with a chorus line at the beginning or end of each stanza.
• Indent each line further than the previous one.
• Set the piece out like a staircase.
• Copy the style of a poem on a similar topic and of similar rhythms and length.

Display the copies of the changed poem around the room and discuss how each form fits the poem. If the prose was originally a poem, show the children the original version and discuss with them the differences between their forms and that chosen by the poet.

### Further activity

Split up a poem or short piece of prose into its constituent sentences and let the children select from these to form a poem. If you use a published poem, let the children see the original after they have devised their own form.

## 18. Gifts

### Age range
Nine and upwards.

### Group size
Small groups and pairs.

### What you need
Paper, pencils.

### What to do
Talk to the children about the gifts bestowed upon Sleeping Beauty at her christening; beauty, wit, grace and the ability to dance, to sing and to make music. Remind them that it was also forewarned that she would prick her finger on a needle and die.

The Magi brought gifts to the infant Christ, showing that he would be a king and a priest, and foretelling his death.

There are many gifts that people would like to bestow upon a baby, gifts that money cannot buy and which are beyond us to give. These are gifts to guide and help the child throughout his life; for example, good health, peace, happiness, love, compassion and tolerance.

Discuss with the children the qualities that they think are important in life, and let them suggest gifts they would like to grant to a new-born child.

Using starter phrases such as 'I give you (the gift of)...', 'I bring you...' or 'You shall...' they can expand on their ideas. The children can then write a number of wishes for the baby, covering different aspects of life.

## Further activity
Ask the children to produce soft crayon drawings to illustrate their gifts, and then to write out their poems on top of the drawings.

# 19. Bequests

### Age range
Nine and upwards.

### Group size
Small groups or pairs.

### What you need
Photocopiable page 182, pencils.

### What to do
Poetry can be used as a means of contemplating the serious side of life. Children are fascinated by death, yet very few have had any experience of it. They need to talk about it and to ask questions. It is normal to want to explore this rite of passage.

Writing wills is a way of looking at the positive side of death, not for monetary gain, but for the joys of life, the quality of human feelings and the recognition of values. Read to the children Hedy-anne Goodman's poem in *What Rhymes with Secret?*, edited by Sandy Brownjohn (Hodder and Stoughton), which ends:

I give you humility,
Practise having it in your
possession.

The children can then write their wills. They could will to others their talents and characteristics as well as their possessions, commenting on whether or not they had been used wisely, and write why this aspect of self is being willed to their friends or family. Useful starter phrases include:
• To you I grant....
• To my ... I bequeath....
• I leave my .....
The children can write out copies of their wills on photocopiable page 182.

# 20. Epitaphs

### Age range
Nine and upwards.

### Group size
Pairs or small groups.

### What you need
Examples of epitaphs, for example from *The Faber Book of Epigrams and Epitaphs*, edited by Geoffrey Grigson, photocopiable page 183, pencils.

## What to do

Epitaphs can make statements about a person's life, character, occupation, attributes or the way they died.

> Here lies the body
> Of Crystabel Blishen,
> Who spent ten years
> Embroidering a cushion.
> She stitched the last stitch,
> And cut the last thread,
> But the sharp scissors
>   slipped
> And she finished up – dead.

This one is from Lydford Village Church in Devon:

> Here lies in horizontal
>   position
> The outside case of
> George Routleigh,
>   Watchmaker.

The epitaph on this tomb is not only a delight to read but well worth close study. The likening of the man to his occupation is brilliantly handled.

Epitaphs are generally serious but those with homophones, homonyms and humour are the ones that appeal to children.

> Let the wind go free
> Wherever it be,
> For 'twas the wind
> That kill-ed me. (Anon)

Epitaphs often rhyme in lines two and four, and occasionally in lines one and three as well. Half-rhymes are sometimes used, as here 'On King Charles the Second' by the Earl of Rochester:

> Here lies our Sovereign Lord
>   the King,
> Whose word no man relies
>   on;
> Who never said a foolish
>   thing,
> Nor ever did a wise one.

Read a number of epitaphs to the children and let them see several examples of the range of approaches before they start composing their own.

They could choose from the following starter phrases:
• Here lies...;
• Here lies the body of...;
• Beneath this stone/sward...;
• In this plot...;
• A (adjective) man was (name)....

The subject could be one of the following:
• a well-known character;
• a fictional one;
• a friend or relative;
• a pet;
• someone in a certain occupation;
• someone who has particular attributes;
• a favourite toy;
• a piece of clothing.

## Further activity

The children can write out their epitaphs on photocopiable page 183.

# 21. Clerihews

## Age range
Nine and upwards.

## Group size
Pairs or small groups.

## What you need
A poetry collection which includes clerihews, a display of clerihews.

## What to do

Clerihews are humorous four-lined rhymes. They are named after their inventor, Edmund Clerihew Bentley. They comprise the simplest form of rhyme possible. Here are some examples by the inventor:

> The Art of Biography
> Is different from Geography.
> Geography is about Maps
> But Biography is about
> Chaps.

> What I like about Clive
> Is that he's no longer alive.
> There's a great deal to be
>    said
> For being dead.

> Sir Christopher Wren
> Said, 'I'm going to dine with
>    some men.
> If anybody calls
> Say I'm designing St Paul's.'
> (Reprinted from *The Complete Clerihews of E. Clerihew Bentley* by permission of Oxford University Press.)

Each clerihew is made up of two pairs of rhyming couplets. The lines can be of any length as it is the rhyme that is all-important, not the rhythm or the length of the syllables. The focus is generally, but not necessarily, a known person.

Read a number of clerihews to the children, and give them an opportunity to read ones on display and in your collection.

Discuss the verses with the class. What do they notice about the form and content? Compose one as a class and write it out on the board.

When the children come to write their own clerihews they will need to remember two things – the rhymes must sound perfectly natural, and the humorous content should be lead by the rhyme.

Make a list of people suggested by the children and look together to see which have humorous possibilities. If a name is difficult to rhyme, use it at the beginning of the first line instead.

While clerihews do not have to be factual or historically accurate, it is amusing to try to create one around something a person is renowned for, as in the clerihew about Sir Christopher Wren.

## Further activity

Encourage the children to write a humorous verse, in clerihew form, about
• a friend;
• a member of the family;
• a sports or television personality;
• the world of nature;
• an aspect of a topic.

# 22. Two-minute poems

## Age range
Ten and upwards.

## Group size
Individuals.

## What you need
A timer, pencils, paper.

## What to do
Writing a two-minute poem means working quickly with quiet concentration.

Virtually any subject is suitable for these poems:
• people;
• animals and pets;
• seasons;
• the sun;
• the night;

- the moon;
- the stars;
- planets;
- space;
- aliens;
- shadows;
- the wind;
- the rain;
- reflections.

When you have told the children the title of the poem, they have just two minutes to scribble down words and ideas that come to mind and write a poem. Encourage the children to think of expressive verbs like 'shattered' and 'cracked', and to be inventive with adjectives, homonyms and homophones.

This focused effort can produce some surprisingly good results because the children are forced to think very quickly in order to encapsulate their ideas.

Do three or four quick poems at any one sitting, sharing them in between each two-minute session. This gives

a break from intense concentration while still focusing on the task.

The children can edit their poems at a later date, if they wish, but the spontaneity must not be lost. Any poems which they feel have been particularly successful can be added to their personal anthologies.

### Further activity
The children can spend two minutes writing about each member of their families. They can then mount the poems on A4 paper with a design that incorporates all the poems. They may like to draw pen portraits as part of the layout.

# 23. Iambics

### Age range
Ten and upwards.

### Group size
Pairs.

### What you need
No special requirements.

### What to do
This activity is concerned with a rhythmic form that reflects the ordinary speech rhythms of English and so lends itself admirably to English poetry.

The iambic rhythm is made up of 'feet'. Each foot has two syllables, a weak beat followed by a strong one as in 'begun' or 'They came...'.

Sonnets have lines with five feet (iambic pentameter), but four-feet lines of seven or eight syllables (iambic tetrameter) are more commonly used in rhymes like 'Jack and Jill' and poetry such as 'A Birthday' by Christina Rossetti:

My heart is like a singing
    bird
Whose nest is in a watered
    shoot;
My heart is like an apple tree
Whose boughs are bent with
    thickset fruit.

or Wordsworth's 'Daffodils':

I wandered lonely as a
    cloud,
That floats on high o'er vales
    and hills ...

Poetry needs rhythm, and iambics are one of the accepted rhythms of poetry. Lewis Carroll highlights their close resemblance to the speech patterns of English in the nonsense rhyme 'The Jabberwocky' from Through the Looking Glass:

Twas brillig and the slithy
  toves
Did gyre and gimble in the
  wabe...

With careful use of
punctuation, the lines of
iambic poetry run on, flowing
naturally from one to the
other. This helps to vary the
feel of the rhythm, and
reduces the temptation to read
each line as if it were an entity
in itself.

To help children get the feel
of the rhythm, have an 'iambic'
session, when only iambic
speech patterns may be used.
Children enjoy these sessions
and quickly catch on to the
rhythm. Through speaking in
iambic rhythms they come to
understand them and use them
naturally in their poetry.

These sessions will lead the
children naturally into
searching for poems written in
iambic rhythm, and will
encourage them to write in
iambics themselves. The way
that iambic verse flows on
from one line to the next,
using natural speech patterns,
leads children's poetry away
from the static rhythms of
early childhood into a more
flowing use of language, yet
retaining a strong inner
rhythm. Iambic verse also
prepares the ground for
writing sonnets.

## Further activity

When the children have the
feel of iambic poetry, if you
think they are ready, introduce
them to other rhythms such as
the following:

**Anapaest**
  When the lights of the
    lounge and the kitchen go
    out,
  And the children asleep in
    their beds...

**Dactyl**
  Five little cakes in the
    bakery shop,
  Spongy inside with a sweet,
    gooey top...

**Trochee**
  Polly put the kettle on....

# CHAPTER 9

# Poetry across the curriculum

Work on poetry can be developed from almost any part of the broad and flexible curriculum that good primary schools provide. Poetry should not be limited to poetry lessons or the language unit in a topic; it should form part of discrete subjects too, extending the language dimension across all curriculum areas. Every subject benefits from close examination, detailed observation and creative thinking, which are all aspects of poetry. For example, the results of a science experiment, translated into poetic form, can bring to light an observation or aspect hitherto unseen.

Experiences in different areas of the curriculum open up new horizons for children, bringing an excitement and involvement which can act as a springboard for poetry. Obviously, poetry lends itself particularly to the study of nature, but also to mathematics, religious education, science, technology, history, geography, art, music and movement.

Too often the written work associated with topics is merely a matter of data collection or regurgitating information. This sort of writing does not encourage children to draw on the knowledge they already have, as poetry does.

# BACKGROUND

Poetry involves writing down what we have found out, collecting together ideas and thoughts, and taking a fresh look at the subject, adding personal experience, feelings and reflection. It also expresses the evanescent qualities of a subject and hints at deeper mysteries in a way that prose writing can not.

When children write in school they are generally telling the teacher something he or she already knows. Through poetry they talk about their experiences differently, uniquely, reflecting the world as it is known to them and them alone.

We must be careful, however, that poetry is not used merely as another way of presenting information, or we will destroy what poetry is and what it can do. Poetry can produce a range of reactions from quiet meditation to laughter. The enjoyment of poetry for its own sake is what we want to preserve.

## Poetry in topic work

The approach to the curriculum changes as children move through the primary school. The youngest children work from topics which enable them to learn from interaction with the environment and with each other. Carefully structured practical activities lay the foundations of key concepts in the various subject disciplines and take up a large part of the day. While much of young children's work is in the oral mode, ideas are also explored through the child's own emergent writing or by using an adult as scribe, until the children are ready to write for themselves.

Children in the middle years often learn from topics which are slanted towards one of the subject disciplines, together with some discrete subject teaching. Top juniors also work from topics strongly biased towards a particular subject, but new national guidelines mean that more time is spent on discrete subject teaching to ensure that all disciplines are covered.

Topics can be based upon a theme from poetry, or poetry can form part of the writing unit of a topic. Poetry can also be used as a way of exploring aspects of discrete curriculum subjects.

Whichever way you work, the themes and topics you use must be ones that excite and interest the children. Whatever the subject of the poetry, children must be able to relate to it. They must be interested enough to *want* to read and write about it. The poetry should grow out of the children's experiences and feelings related to the subject, but there will be times when you will need to supply extra help and ideas, because children, like adults, have days when their heads seem to be empty of ideas.

## Techniques for topic poems

### Word heaps
Use a word heap to give direction to a brainstorming session. You can either make your own, based upon the topic you have in mind, or use the one on photocopiable page 184.

Select any five consecutive words from the word heap, and write them down. The word order can be changed to make it more coherent, and the words themselves may also be changed slightly. What do the children think the words suggest? What ideas spring from the chosen words? Write their ideas down, one beneath the other, and begin to explore them through the images they create and the feelings they evoke. The aim is to write down as many words as possible in a brainstorming session of five minutes. The children can then work together to turn their list of words into a poem.

### All sorts of lists
There are a number of ways of using lists to help in writing topic-based poems:
• Give the children one word connected with the topic, and then ask them to write down, without stopping to think, any and every word that comes to mind. You will find some very interesting juxtapositions of similar words, connected words and opposites. Sometimes there is no connection between one word and the next, in which case the mind has made an unexpected leap, and a little right-brain initiative has been let in!
• Write one list of all the words the children can think of connected with an *aspect* of the theme. Write a second list of all the words connected with a *feeling* aroused by it. Use these two lists to create a poem.
• Divide the paper into five columns and head each one with the name of one of the senses. Under each heading list the words that describe that aspect of the theme.
• Ask the children for aspects or attributes of the theme that come to mind. For example, on the theme of the sun, they might proffer words like heat, light, colour, power. Select four attributes which each encompass a wide area of the topic, and then fold a piece of paper into four and use one attribute to head each of the columns. The children can then list appropriate words in the columns.
• Mapping or spider-grams: write the word in the centre of the page and surround it with words that come to mind. These then spawn other satellites or clusters of words.

Vary the way the lists are made, so that the children learn to select the form of list most suited to their purpose.

List-making is a way of focusing thoughts and bringing associated words to the forefront of the mind. As children's writing speed increases, a list becomes a stream of consciousness and, from the unconscious patterning of words, unexpected connections occur which give rise to ideas.

When they have finished, let the children look for words in their lists that rhyme, or that have a similar rhythm. They can also begin to group words together because they express an idea or are harmonious. Then they can start to order the lines and phrases to make a poem.

### List poems

The following poems explore list forms:
• 'Pockets' by Brian Lee in *A Shooting Star*, collected by Wes Magee (Blackwell).
• 'Christmas Stocking' by Eleanor Farjeon in *A Christmas Stocking*, compiled by Wes Magee (Cassell).
• 'Weather is Full of the Nicest Sounds' by Aileen Fisher in *My Red Poetry Book* and 'Full of the Moon' in *My Blue Poetry Book*, both edited by Moira Andrew (Macmillan).
• 'Fight of the Year' by Roger McGough in *Watchwords* by Peter and Michael Benton (Hodder and Stoughton).

• 'I Want a Sandwich' by Remy Charlip in *A World of Poetry*, selected by Michael Rosen (Kingfisher Books).

### Jottings and doodles

Let the children doodle, draw or make jottings while you read them a story or prose passage connected with work in any part of the curriculum. They must not do anything that will distract anyone's attention away from the story, but they can draw or make notes as words come to mind. By the end of the story the children will have a collection of words, phrases and drawings.

Discuss the words they have written. Why did those particular ones come to the children's minds? Write the more interesting ones on the board and work with the children to make the list into a poem. Try to keep away from the story, if you can, so that the children see how the words can spark off completely new ideas and follow a different tack. You can take a single moment out of the story, but do not make the poem a retelling or résumé.

When the children start to write on their own, some will be ready to explore their words in the way that you have done, but others may want to retell the story as a narrative poem in rhyming couplets or quatrains. For some this is because of the story's appeal, but more often it is because it is safer – the story line and form are already there to guide their writing. However, this is a starting point from which they will grow away – with experience and support.

When the children mount their poems or write them in their anthologies they can use their doodling as ideas for illustrations.

### Using the themes

Most of the themes dealt with in this chapter could become topics in themselves; links with other curriculum areas will probably spring readily to mind. If you want to use the activities as springboards for wider topic work, please do so, but there should also be the opportunity for poetry to grow out of a specific activity without necessarily forming part of a larger project.

# ACTIVITIES

## Science

The most effective approach to teaching science is an investigative one. Investigation includes exploration of the children's immediate environment, first-hand experiences, manipulation of objects and materials, and close observation, all of which are valuable aids for writing good poetry. Comparison of one thing with another leads to writing poems containing similes and metaphors, while questioning things and arguing about them will allow deeper investigation to take place.

These skills help to increase children's vocabulary and communication skills, as well as developing their awareness of, interest in and concern for their world.

The children need to make notes as an observer, writing about the colours, smells, shapes and textures of the natural world as well as their thoughts and responses. They should list what they already know about the subject, what they have found out, and their feelings about the subject. They can use all this information to write a poem. You may wish to prescribe the form or leave it open, depending on the topic.

Encourage the children to use magnifying glasses, microscopes and binoculars to look at aspects of nature, and then to write about what they see, using words and short phrases.

Science is a process of personal observation, thinking and investigation which should be articulated, in the early years, through expressive language which is also personal and exploratory. Later, children will record what they have done in straightforward terms. They can then respond to the fact they have recorded in an expressive mode such as poetry. Here are two stanzas from Adrian's poem written after dissecting a frog:

> Like a small child
> pulling apart a toy
> he cannot mend,
> I dissected the frog....
>
> The frog back in its bag,
> My hands washed clean of
> the smell of formalin,
> I eat my dinner.

Science has many aspects, too broad to be covered here, but the following activities offer suggestions and approaches for using poetry in a scientific context.

## 1. Seeing

### Age range
Five to six as a class activity; seven and upwards in groups.

### Group size
Any.

### What you need
Pictures of signs, symbols, advertisements, appealing photographs or pictures cut from colour supplements, magazines and old calendars. Mount these pictures on card and cover them with transparent plastic film or laminate them.

### What to do
Children need to be helped to *see* as well as to look. In this visual world they are surrounded by stimuli: signs, symbols, advertisements, pictures and the omnipresent television. As a consequence

children look at more but see less; in other words, images are recorded by the eyes but very little of what has been observed is registered by the brain.

Children need to be helped to understand and register what they see. When they say 'I like that' or 'That's nice' or 'Look at that' – what is it that they like about it? Why does it look 'nice'? What are the qualities that appeal to their senses? Are they reacting to the colour, line, texture and shape separately or in combination with each other?

By making a note of particular things they see, children will begin to look at specifics. There are a number of ways they can do this:

• They can make a four-column list and head the columns 'colour', 'line', 'texture' and 'shape'. Under each heading they should state the detail that attracts. From these lists a poem can be made.

• They can write an 'I like' poem. Younger children can begin each line with 'I like the...', while older children should be encouraged to identify attractive features more specifically: 'I like the colour of...'; I like the shape...' and so on.

• They can write an 'I don't like' poem in the same way.

• They can write a descriptive poem. On the first line they should define what the poem is about. They could begin with 'I am...' or 'Here is a...', or simply 'The...'. Suitable natural subjects for such a poem could be a piece of fruit, a flower, a season or a creature, and so on.

• They could consider the use of colour in the natural world, for example, for camouflage or warning. They should write where the subject of their poem is found, what it is about its appearance that is important – its capacity to hide, to attract or to repel – and what is appealing or distasteful about it. Consider also the other aspects of colour; cool and warm colours, colours that represent different moods, such as red for anger, orange for warmth and yellow for happiness.

## Further activities

Use all the following stimuli to help children write in a detailed way about what they observe.

• Display poems that explore the senses. Put out jars of smells, textures to touch, things to taste and objects to observe, along with magnifying glasses and microscopes.

• The children can make flowers with cotton wool centres and scent them with essential oils and pungent flavourings.

• Cook together and discuss the smells, sights, tastes and textures.

• Explore sounds with tuned and untuned instruments, and record street sounds, animal sounds and playground sounds.

# 2. Winter

### Age range
Five to six as a class activity; seven and upwards in small groups.

### Group size
The whole class, small groups, pairs and individuals.

### What you need
Snowy weather, a range of winter poems.

### What to do
There's nothing like a few flakes of snow to bring wild excitement to the classroom. Capitalise on it! Tell the children to put their coats on and go outside. How do the snowflakes feel on the hand, on the tongue? A child in my class once wrote that snow tasted like 'wet sherbet' and I know just what she meant.

Read the following poems about snow with the children:
• 'Winter' and 'December' by Judith Nicholls in *Midnight Forest* (Faber and Faber).
• 'Snow in December' by Judith Nicholls in *Magic Mirror* (Faber and Faber).
• 'The Snowman' by Ruth Ainsworth and 'Snow' by Ian Mcmillan and Martyn Wiley in *My Red Poetry Book*, edited by Moira Andrew (Macmillan).
• 'Winter Morning' by Ogden Nash and 'Icicle Joe' by Jean Kenward in *My Violet Poetry Book*, edited by Moira Andrew (Macmillan).

Prepare the children for writing poems by making a word list. Use it for short poems such as acrostics, similes, metaphors, haiku and other syllabic forms.

Mount the poems on paper snowflakes as part of a winter scene, with icicles made from white paper.

Add copies of the children's favourite published winter poems, written in their best handwriting and illustrated suitably.

# 3. Minibeasts

## Age range
Five to six as a class activity; seven and upwards in groups.

## Group size
The whole class, small groups, pairs and individuals.

## What you need
Magnifying glasses, clear plastic containers, lids with air holes, water spray, paper, a collection of poems about minibeasts.

## What to do
Go for a minibeast hunt around the school grounds. Turn over stones and let the children look at the minibeasts underneath with a magnifying glass.

Put some damp soil and pebbles in a clear plastic container and spray the soil with water. Carefully place the minibeast into the container and cover the container with a lid with air holes. The minibeasts can then be taken indoors for closer observation. (**NB** Remember to return the creatures to their natural environment as soon as the children have finished studying them, no later than the end of the day.)

The children should choose one of the creatures to study and note its shape, length, colour, thickness and movement. They could make an observational drawing of the creature and look for poems about it. What do the poems include beside the basic description? Why?

The following poems may be useful:
• 'Spider's Song' by Judith Nicholls in *Magic Mirror* (Faber and Faber).
• 'Who's There?' and 'Woodlouse' by Judith Nicholls in *Midnight Forest* (Faber and Faber).
• Nursery rhyme: 'Ladybird, ladybird, fly away home'.
• 'Dragonfly' by John Cotton, 'Snails' by Tony Charles, 'Insects' by J. Walsh, and 'Daddy Longlegs' by Geoffrey Holloway in *Language in Colour*, edited by Moira Andrew (Belair).
• 'Centipedes' by Martin Honeysett in *Another First Poetry Book*, compiled by John Foster (Oxford University Press).
• 'Dragonfly' by Jean Kenward in *The Unicorn and Lions*, edited by Moira Andrew (Macmillan).

Next they should decide the shape for the poem. Should it echo the shape or the movement of the creature? Snails with their spiral shells and worms with their wiggly movements are wonderful for shape poems.

• 'Crickets' by Valerie Worth in *Marbles in my Pocket*, edited by Moira Andrew (Macmillan).
• 'Snail' by Pam Gidney, 'Caterpillar-Keeper' by Libby Houston, 'Grasshopper' by Jean Kenward in *Go and Open the Door*, edited by Moira Andrew (Macmillan).
• 'Drowsy Flies' by Rodney Bennett, 'The Ladybird' by Clive Sansom, 'Silverfish, Spiders and Flies' by Stanley Cook, 'The Wolf Spider' by R.C. Scriven, all in *A Shooting Star*, collected by Wes Magee (Blackwell).

Ask the children to make a list of words and phrases that describe their minibeast. Once they have done this they can decide the sort of poem they want to write and the form it should take.

## 4. Butterflies

### Age range
Six and upwards.

### Group size
The whole class, pairs and individuals.

### What you need
Poems about butterflies, thick powder paint, brushes, sheets of A4 paper, adhesive, pale blue paper.

### What to do
Encourage the children to make a 'blob' painting using bright colours. They should drop blobs of paint along the centre crease of an A4 sheet of paper and then fold the paper in half and smooth out the

paint, pressing outwards from the centre crease.

Somehow the finished painting often turns out to be butterfly-shaped, but if not, you can trim it to shape. The children should cut out their 'butterflies', fold them along the body line, and stick them on to a pale blue background. They can then surround their butterflies with relevant words and phrases. Older children can find and write these for themselves, but you may need to scribe for younger children. Encourage them to use alliteration and assonance.

Select one of the 'blob' butterflies to work with the class and create a poem. Older children can work alone or in pairs, using their own pictures.

The following are some further suggestions for developing butterfly poems:
• The children could draw a butterfly in outline and 'paint' in its wings with descriptive words and phrases like 'honey brown', 'brilliant blue', 'showy', 'golden hues', 'jewelled colours', 'delicate', 'zigzag', 'fluttering'. They can then use these words to create a poem.
• Older children can work from a model or detailed picture of a butterfly or visit a butterfly farm. Encourage the children to write a haiku, a cinquain or a quatrain, making an observational drawing first. As

descriptive words come to mind while the children are drawing, they can 'map' these words on another piece of paper. By the time the children come to write they will know so much about the butterfly they have been observing that their thinking and observation begin to coalesce and the poem is easier to write. This technique can of course be used for writing poems on other subjects.

• The children could write a poem with the following format. First write the name (butterfly), then two adjectives, two verbs and a synonym for the name. This gives a total of six words which should gradually build up a picture of the creature and how the writer feels about it.

> Butterfly
> Blue butterfly
> Beautiful, blue butterfly
> Beautiful, blue butterfly
>     hovering,
> Beautiful, blue butterfly
>     hovering, fluttering,
> Lepidoptera.

Read the following poems about butterflies:
• 'Butterflies Cry' by Felix Redmill, 'Chrysalis' by Muriel Spark and 'Butterfly Calypso' by Irene Rawnsley in *Go and Open the Door* chosen by Moira Andrew (Macmillan).
• 'Butterfly' by Stanley Cook in *Another First Poetry Book* chosen by John Foster (Oxford University Press).

• Various poems from *I Like That Stuff* collected by Morag Styles (Cambridge University Press).

### Further activities
Devise a garden mural with paintings of grasses and flowers. Mount the poems and butterfly pictures on the mural. Alternatively, the children can write their poems, along with copies of published ones, in a 'Butterfly poetry book'.

# 5. Flying

### Age range
Six and upwards.

### Group size
The whole class, pairs and individuals.

### What you need
Pictures of anything that flies; seeds from sycamore, ash and maple trees, an old telephone directory, card, paper-clips, sticky tape, squares of fabric, plastic sheeting, tissue paper and other papers, cotton-reels and other small weights, cotton thread.

### What to do
Encourage the children to make paper planes from pages taken from an old telephone directory. They can study the different ways the gliders fly when they are: flown indoors; flown from a height; flown outdoors on a still day and flown outdoors on a windy day. What happens if they weight the nose of the glider with a paper-clip?

The children can also make a spinner as shown in the diagram below. They should add a paper-clip to the part that hangs down and drop it from shoulder height. If they change the position of the paper-clip, what effect does this have?

The children could also make parachutes by taking a square piece of fabric, plastic or tissue paper, tying the four corners with pieces of thread to make a canopy and knotting

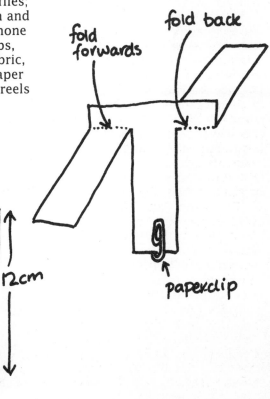

the threads through a cotton-reel. They should make canopies of different sizes, using a range of materials, and attach different weights to investigate how this affects the time and distance of flight.

Ask the children to note down any words, phrases and thoughts that come to mind while they are making and flying the gliders, spinners and parachutes. They can use these when they are writing up the experiments.

When they have described what they did the children can write a poem, adding to the factual description how they felt and what they thought while it was happening.

## Further activities
• A visit to the RAF museum at Middle Wallop, or to another similar museum, can be enthralling for some children and will give rise to some exciting poetry.
• Talk about what it would be like to float over the world, silently, hearing a range of different sounds, seeing the world from a different perspective and feeling remote from normal life. The children could write a descriptive poem about what it would be like to have the power of flight.
• Read the following poems with the children: 'Boy flying' by Leslie Norris and 'Floating Stuff' by John Lees in *The Unicorn and Lions*, edited by Moira Andrew (Macmillan); 'Wings' by Pie Corbett in *Another First Poetry Book*, compiled by John Foster (Oxford University Press).

# 6. Kites

## Age range
Seven and upwards.

## Group size
The whole class, small groups, pairs or individuals.

## What you need
A polystyrene ceiling tile, two buttons about 2cm in diameter, a heavier button about 4cm in diameter, string, coloured paper, thread, cord, photocopiable page 185.

## What to do
Show the children how to make a kite by making one hole in the centre of the polystyrene tile and another hole about 12cm above it, as shown in the diagram. Stick a small button over the top of each hole to prevent the tile tearing in the wind and thread a piece of string through the buttons. Make a loop by threading both ends of the string through a heavy button and tying a knot, as shown. The children can then tie on a towing line, affix streamers made from coloured paper, and the kite is ready to fly.

Using photocopiable page 185, the children can write on the smaller ties any words and phrases which arose as they made and flew their kites, and write mini-poems or haiku on the larger ties.

## Further activities
• Ask the children to paint pictures of kites and stick them on to a colour-washed pale blue paper. They can also add longer poems to this display.
• The children could write their poems on kites made from brightly coloured paper, and suspend them by threads from cords hung across the classroom so that they twist and turn in the air.

# 7. Links in a chain

## Age range
Seven and upwards.

## Group size
Small groups, pairs, individuals.

## What you need
Examples of life cycles, seasons, food chains and other recurring themes in nature; examples of different kinds of chains.

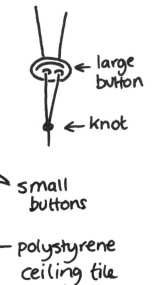

large button

knot

small buttons

polystyrene ceiling tile

large button

## What to do

Show the children a variety of different types of chains, so that they can see how a chain is made from links. Show them how to make a paper chain by threading each strip of paper through the loop made by the previous one. Use a thin paper strip to join two chains made from strong paper and show how, when the chain is pulled, the weak link breaks.

Talk about how things grow from seeds. Grow some cress on wet blotting paper or in half an egg-shell with a face painted on it. Talk about the food we grow, how some of it is good for humans and other parts feed other animals.

Read 'Black Dot' by Libby Houston in *Word Games* by Sandy Brownjohn and Janet Whitaker (Hodder and Stoughton), and 'Chrysalis' by Muriel Spark in *Go and Open and Door*, edited by Moira Andrew (Macmillan).

Discuss life cycles with the children, such as those of the frog or the butterfly. They can draw these out and write poems about them. Here is a poem, written in rhyming couplets, which grew out of class work on food chains.

Display the children's poems beside the relevant natural chains, cycles or patterns.

*Food chain*

After his wives have slain
    the prey,
The Lord of the Pride dines
    all day.

When the lion's had enough
The lionesses snarl and
    stuff.

When the ladies admit
    defeat
The mischievous cubs tear
    at the treat.

When the cubs have gorged
    their gut,
The gaunt hyenas come
    sauntering up.

When the hyenas have
    wolfed their fill
The hungry vultures accost
    the kill.

When the vultures have
    winged away
The army of ants has a field
    day.

And when the swarming ants
    are done,
The bones are bleached by
    the broiling sun.

## Further activities

• Do an experiment on water evaporation and condensation in class and ask the children to write a chain poem about its cyclic qualities.
• Ask the children to write a poem about the seasons, to show life, death and regeneration in the natural world. (Synonyms, metaphors and kennings lend themselves to this theme.)

# History

History is about people, the events in their lives and the things that affected them. For recent history especially, there are many artefacts which children can see and touch, and streets they can walk along to bring them in touch with the people and events of the past. All these things can make wonderful stimuli for poetry.

Although the people of the past are distanced from us by time, as well as by their attitudes and way of life, poetry helps history to come alive in an active, immediate way. History asks 'Why...?', 'I wonder what it was like to...'. Through poetry children can develop these thoughts, deepening their knowledge and understanding.

Poetry explores history in a number of ways, helping children to form impressions from those who have looked, listened and experienced before. Various sorts of poetry are particularly useful in a historical context:

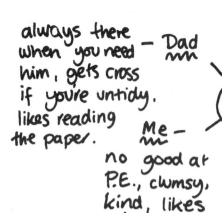

always there
when you need — **Dad**
him, gets cross
if you're untidy,
likes reading
the paper.　**Me** —
no good at
P.E., clumsy,
kind, likes
writing and
reading

**Mum** — always very busy, worried,
rushing, likes bright colours
reading, crosswords.

**PORTER**

**Liz** — funny, bright, likes
eating kidney (!), has
tons of friends

**Greg** — understanding,
laughs loudly,
gets cross easily

These are just a few ideas. Once you start thinking about poetry in terms of social, economic and political history, both you and the children will discover many examples.

# 1. My family

### Age range
Five and upwards.

### Group size
The whole class and individuals.

### What you need
Large sheets of paper, thick felt-tipped pens.

### What to do
Talk with the children about families, and the differences and similarities between them. Ask the children about the members of their families and things they particularly notice about them.

Read poems like the following:
• 'Aunt Flo' by John Cotton from *Over the Bridge*, edited by John Loveday (Puffin).
• 'My Dad' by Maureen Natt, 'Pearls' by Jean Little and 'My Baby Brother' by Ian Aitken in *A World of Poetry*, selected by

Michael Rosen (Kingfisher).
• 'My Father's Hands' by Jeni Couzyn in *The Unicorn and Lions*, edited by Moira Andrew (Macmillan).

Ask the children to map their family, by writing their family name in the middle of a sheet of paper and then, radiating out from this, the names of each member of the family. The children can write appropriate words beside each name, describing the people, writing phrases that distinguish them from other members of the family: 'always dropping things', 'hair stiff, like a lavatory brush', 'hands messy with paints', 'floury nose'. With younger children you can do this activity as a class, using generic terms rather than names – 'mother', 'father', 'brother', 'sister' and so on.

A range of poetry can come from this map of information. Older children could try cinquains, writing the relationship as the one-word first line and ending with the person's name or an appropriate word for the last line. Here's what Charlotte wrote about her mother:

Mum
Gentle, happy,
Dusts, hoovers, cleans,
Kind, thoughtful, loving,
　caring,
Caroline.

• narrative poems tell of events and people;
• sea shanties and other work songs tell about living and working in the past;
• nursery rhymes and chants remind us of historical events – 'Ring-a-ring of roses' explores the Great Plague of 1665, and 'Remember, remember the fifth of November' has obvious historical connotations;
• biographical poems, both serious and funny, tell us about famous figures;
• sonnets tell us about the social mores of their time;
• poems of the First and Second World Wars tell of hardship, pain, suffering, inner feelings and precious moments;
• poems about inventions, discoveries and explorations recount new ideas and opinions;
• poems about food and farming explore the changing styles of living, working and eating;
• religious poems speak of different faiths.

## 2. Family history

### Age range
Five and upwards.

### Group size
The whole class and individuals.

### What you need
Old photographs of previous generations of the children's families.

### What to do
Ask the children to bring to school the oldest family photographs they can. As these may well be treasured items, invite parents to bring them in for you to take care of. You may be fortunate enough to receive some photographs taken at the end of the last century to talk about.

Look together at the clothes, the situations and the people that are present. How much do the photographs tell of life in those times? The children can use the information gained from the photographs and from talks with their grandparents, to write a descriptive poem about one of their relatives. Children who do not have an old photograph can write about an incident told to them by an elderly relative, or write an imaginary poem about 'My Great-Granny'.

Read poems like the following:

• 'My Mother Saw a Dancing Bear' by Charles Causley in *Figgie Hobbin* (Puffin).
• 'My Grandmother' by Elizabeth Jennings and 'Aunt Julia' by Norman MacCaig in *The Unicorn and Lions*, edited by Moira Andrew (Macmillan).
• 'Uncle William' by Judith Nicholls in *Magic Mirror* (Faber and Faber).

## 3. Christmas

### Age range
Five to seven as a class activity; eight and upwards in groups.

### Group size
Any.

### What you need
A collection of Christmas poems, both religious and secular.

### What to do
Read the children a range of Christmas poems such as the following:
• 'The Wicked Singers' by Kit Wright, 'It's Christmas' by Wes Magee, 'Welcome' (Anon), and 'High in the Heaven' by Charles Causley in *A Shooting Star*, collected by Wes Magee (Blackwell).

• 'Christmas Eve' by Brian Levison and 'The Christmas Tree' by John Walsh in *My Violet Poetry Book*, edited by Moira Andrew (Macmillan).
• 'What Does Christmas Mean to Me' by Brian Levison in *My Red Poetry Book*, edited by Moira Andrew (Macmillan).
• 'Room at the Inn' by Judith Nicholls in her collection *Midnight Forest* (Faber and Faber).
• 'In the Bleak Mid-winter' by Christina Rossetti in *A Puffin Book of Verse*, compiled by Eleanor Graham.

Display a picture of Mary, Joseph, Jesus and their visitors and ask the children for words relating to the picture. Use these words to create a list poem, a seasonal poem or a celebratory poem.

Write the letters of the word Christmas down the side of a sheet of paper, and ask the children for Christmassy words for each letter, to make an acrostic.

With older children use 'Stable Song' by Judith Nicholls

in *Magic Mirror* (Faber and Faber) for study. What is the main idea? How is it explored? Look at the use of repeated lines. What effect does that have on the composition of the poem, and on the reader? What effect does the poem have on different members of the class?

### Further activities
• Make a collection of Christmas poems and intersperse the children's own poems with published ones.
• Use the children's poems as part of a Christmas display.
• Find a poem you all enjoy and perform it as a class at a festive concert.
• Ask the children to design Christmas cards and write mini-poems or short four-line verses to go inside.
• Let the children make stars and write haiku or mini-poems in them. They could spread the edges with adhesive and sprinkle the stars with glitter.

# 4. Railways

### Age range
Eight and upwards.

### Group size
Any.

### What you need
A collection of poems about trains.

### What to do
Poems about railways and trains usually have a strong, relentless rhythm so that the reader gets a feeling of the speed and rhythm of a train, for example:

> Faster than fairies, faster
>     than witches,
> Bridges and houses, hedges
>     and ditches....
> (from R.L. Stevenson's 'From
> a Railway Carriage')

Organise a class trip on a steam train, perhaps at the North Somerset Railway or the Bluebell Railway in Sussex. This will help the children to feel the rhythm for themselves. Visit the Railway Museum in York, the Science Museum in London or the Open Air Museum at Beamish in County Durham to enable the children to get a sense of a train's size and power.

Together with the children, find, read and make a collection of train poems. Encourage the children to feel the rhythm by tapping it out using untuned percussion instruments. Display the train poems with pictures and posters of trains and railways to continue the visual impact.

Ask the children to keep a note of words and phrases that come to mind as they look at the trains. They should consider the other senses too! They can write their poems using these words, perhaps borrowing rhythms from published poems about trains, for example:
• W.H. Auden's 'The Night Mail' in *More Word Games* by Sandy Brownjohn and Janet Whitaker (Hodder and Stoughton).
• 'From a Railway Carriage' by R.L. Stevenson in *The Oxford Treasury of Children's Poems* (Oxford University Press).
• 'Midnight on the Great Western' by Thomas Hardy.
• 'Trains' by James S. Tippett in *Dragon's Smoke*, edited by Wes Magee (Blackwell).

# 5. Vikings

### Age range
Nine and upwards.

### Group size
The whole class and small groups.

### What you need
'Night Attack' by Gregory Harrison in his collection *Posting Letters* (Oxford University Press), split into eight sections, with one section for each group; a collection of pictures, resource books, stories, myths and legends about the Vikings.

### What to do

Gregory Harrison's poem tells the story, through the eyes of a young man looking back, of an unsuccessful raid on his village by the Danes. Although many were killed, he and his mother escaped. The poem falls neatly into eight sections.

Do not talk about the poem in advance, or tell the children that it is about a Viking attack. See what period or event they come up with.

Divide your class into eight groups and give each group one section of the poem. Ask them to discuss:
• what is happening in their section;
• what they think led up to their section;
• what it is likely to be leading on to.

Each group should then report back with their answers to the questions. Discuss the stories the groups come up with and their closeness to the original. Many sections of the poem could describe a number of tragic historical events, so it is interesting to see how the children interpret them.

The language in this poem is evocative, making good use of sensory images, as here:

The black hooved rumble of
     the smoke
The yellow snarl of flame
The bubbled plop of resin
     boiled
On blistered doorway frame.

### Further activity

The groups can work together to write a narrative poem concentrating on one aspect of the Vikings, perhaps a victorious homecoming, their faith, festivals, myths or a ballad about the life of a slave. Children will need to research the facts and weave them into the poem, so see that the necessary background books and stories are available to them.

## 6. Fire!

### Age range
Nine and upwards.

### Group size
The whole class.

### What you need
Paper, matches, a candle, tongs, a dish, a bucket of water.

### What to do
Use this activity to establish the atmosphere for work on the Great Fire of London in 1666.

Take every precaution against fire! Make sure there are no draughts, that nothing flammable is nearby and that a bucket of water is beside you.

Work in front of the children. Light the candle and hold a piece of paper with the tongs. Let it just touch the candle flame, then pull it away. Do this several times around the edge of the paper, and then hold the paper over the flame so that a small hole is burned in the centre of the paper. Catch any burned pieces in a dish.

Supervise one group at a time as they char some paper in the controlled area so that they can hear, smell and see what happens. After the experience they can write a poem about fire.

Once redrafting has been completed, the children should write their poems on their pieces of charred paper, and mount them on a fiery background. Here are some display ideas:
• Paint a bonfire scene and arrange the poems as if exploding from it.
• Mount the poems so that the paper is curved or twisted rather than flat.
• Paint a colour wash over the backing paper, starting with red at the bottom or on the horizon, and fading through orange and yellow to grey, with black smoky clouds at the top.

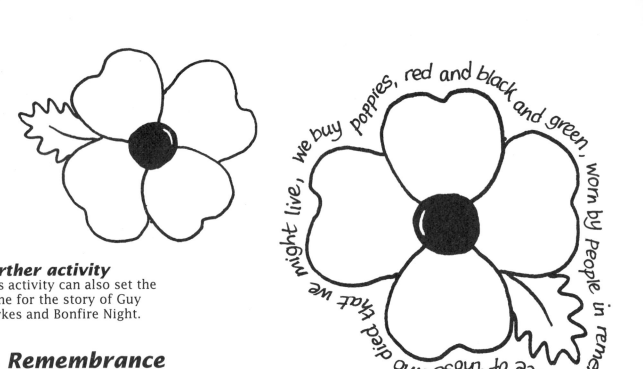

## Further activity
This activity can also set the scene for the story of Guy Fawkes and Bonfire Night.

# 7. Remembrance

### Age range
Nine and upwards.

### Group size
Individuals and pairs.

### What you need
A poppy, information about the two World Wars.

### What to do
As part of a project on the First and Second World Wars, or because it is the time of year (or both) talk with the children about the meaning of Remembrance Day. The children could ask older relatives or neighbours for personal reminiscences of the war. A visit to an old persons' day centre or home may bring personal details which add depth to the children's writing. They can use their notes from such a visit to write articles, stories and poems.

Encourage the children to experiment with loop poems.

These are written around the outside of a picture to form a complete circle. Ross drew a poppy and wrote a loop poem around the outside, as shown in the illustration above.

Often, as here, children's loop poems will indicate a moving away from the set rhymes and rhythms of early childhood. The poetry has yet to develop the internal rhythm of free verse, but no longer are lines forced to rhyme.

### Further activity
Prayers based around the same theme can be in the form of prose or poetry. Colin's prayer is simple and direct:

Dear Lord God,
Help us remember
those who fought
in the war for us.

Make sure that we
never forget
their sacrifice.
Amen.

# Geography

Geography is about places, maps, routes, features of the landscape, the immediate locality and the wider world. It is about weather, climate, rivers and oceans, landforms and the animals they support.

Geographical work with young children involves themes such as finding their way to school or to the local shops, street names, local place names, local industry, and the landscape close to where the children live. Even quite young children can consider how all these things affect the life of the area. Later they will discover similar things in the world outside their home town.

Poetry can use themes like 'On my way to school', and consider the local shops and their window displays – greengrocery has lovely colours, tastes and smells to write about. Other geographical themes include landscape and weather – walking in the rain, scuffing through the autumn leaves, considering storms, floods and drought. There can even be poetry in the names of stations on the local railway line.

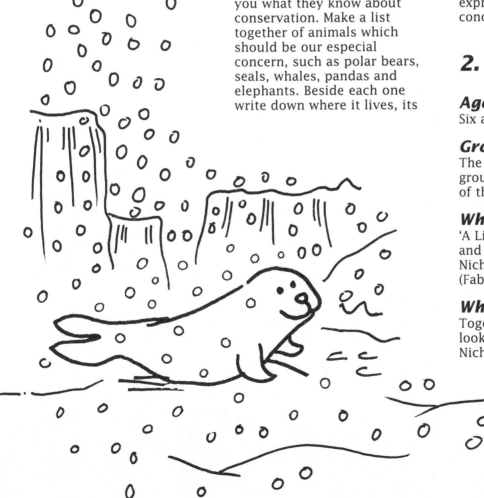

# 1. Prayers for protection

### Age group
Five and upwards.

### Group size
The whole class or small groups.

### What you need
A flipchart or large sheets of paper, pens, pencils, paper.

### What to do
Environmental concern needs to be established early in children's minds. Talk to the children and get them to tell you what they know about conservation. Make a list together of animals which should be our especial concern, such as polar bears, seals, whales, pandas and elephants. Beside each one write down where it lives, its needs and the things we should be concerned about to protect it.

Older children can work together in groups, but it is best if you work with young children, using large sheets of paper or a flipchart. Write the name of one animal on the sheet. Write on it the words already suggested and ask the children to give you phrases to describe the creature, its habitat, its needs and the dangers it faces.

Write a prayer together expressing these concerns. The prayers are most effective if they are short, so you will need to work with the children to edit their prayer in order to express their concerns concisely.

# 2. Name rhymes

### Age range
Six and upwards.

### Group size
The whole class or smaller groups, depending on the age of the children.

### What you need
'A Lincolnshire Nursery Rhyme' and 'Poached Egg' by Judith Nicholls, from *Midnight Forest* (Faber and Faber).

### What to do
Together with the children, look at the poems by Judith Nicholls, which use the rhythm

of well-known nursery rhymes. Using names of local streets or nearby suburbs or villages, the children can make copy-cat poems to the rhythm of either 'Humpty Dumpty' or 'Jack and Jill'.

The children need to be able to tap out the rhythm of the rhymes confidently. It may help to write out the rhythm using long stokes (—) to represent stressed beats and short strokes (–) to represent lighter ones.

Next the children should find local names that fit the rhythm, looking especially for any that rhyme or half-rhyme to go at the ends of the second and fourth lines.

When the children are happy with their version, display the original nursery rhyme together with the children's verse.

### Further activity
The children can choose a different rhyme and fit to it the names of places in a particular country they are studying in geography. Sometimes the children get carried away with this idea, and you may be able to make up a booklet of their name rhymes.

## 3. Volcanoes

### Age range
Ten and upwards.

### Group size
Pairs and individuals.

### What you need
Pictures, stories and poems about volcanoes.

### What to do
Studying volcanoes brings vivid images to children's

minds. It can be useful to provide them with an opportunity to express these ideas in poetry.

The poems will provide evidence of what a child has understood and taken in from the work. Carl's poem, for example, shows his level of understanding and his ability to express the knowledge he has acquired.

*An Island Is Born*

When the rumbling ceased
   echoing,
And the guts of the
   mountain slept silently,
Twitching a little,
Beneath the cover of the
   untroubled sea,
Below the giant torso of this
   terror,
Lies pools of steaming
   magma,
Almost bursting to get out of
   its imprisonment,
A loud crack releases the
   magma from its cell,
Spurting up through the
   rock,
It cuts through the head of
   the monstrous volcano,
The sea turns red as blood,
Boiling on a stove,
It rises up to meet the sky,
And an island is born.

Carl's poem was typed and printed out using a word processor. This often helps to give the child a sense that his or her work has been published.

## Personal and social education

Many aspects of personal and social education should be discussed in the classroom, and teachers may identify a need to explore specific elements in greater detail. Thoughts and feelings about society and relationships often lend themselves to deeper expression through poetry.

How children think and feel about themselves has repercussions for everything

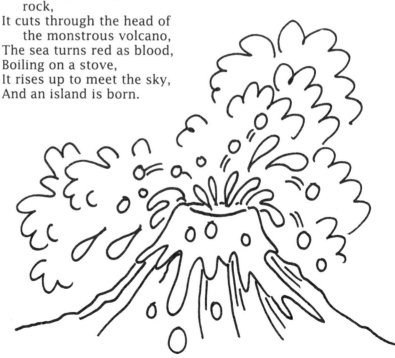

they do, including their ability to make and keep friends and to cope with conflict and aggression. An outlet needs to be provided for these feelings and concerns in a way that is non-threatening. Children need to be allowed to explore and consider their thoughts and opinions, and to compare them with those of others. Through discussion and reading each other's work children will come to understand that they are not alone in their anxieties; others share them too.

# 1. Feelings

## Age range
Five to seven as a class activity; seven and upwards in groups.

## Group size
The whole class, pairs or individuals.

## What you need
A large sheet of paper and felt-tipped pens or a chalkboard and chalk; a range of photographs; poetry anthologies.

## What to do
Writing is easiest for children if they are allowed to express their own concerns, things they know and care about. Through poetry they can often express emotions deep inside them that would not come out in any other way.

Photographs from the press or from companies like Philip Green Educational (see page 173) often provide the jumping-off point for a discussion. Select pictures which suggest a range of emotions, and use open-ended questions. What do the children think is happening in the picture? Why? How would they feel if...?

Have a 'search' session, a time spent reading through the poetry anthologies looking for poems that express a particular emotion. While doing this children will probably be sidetracked by other poems they come across. It's important to be understanding about this, but

keep them close to the main task by giving them a fixed time in which to find at least two poems.

Ask the children to read some of the poems they have found to the class. If you feel it is appropriate, you can lead into writing from here.

With one class of ten-year-olds, a discussion on things that make us feel sad led to some insightful work from the class. Just two examples give an indication of the range of different treatments of the theme. Justian, a keen sportsman, communicates his feelings in a mature way and asks us to reach behind the lines into his thinking:

*My Magnificent Swim*

I get out of the pool,
And wipe my face.
I look up and see a man.
I say to him 'I swam a mile'.

He says to me,
'How many lengths is that?'
'Thirty-two' I say to him.
'I know a boy' he says to me
'Who can swim ninety-three.'

Lois is more altruistic and raises an issue she feels strongly about, too strongly to be able to stand back from it and effect any redrafting:

Hatred running through my
    veins,
Sitting in the edge of my
    seat,
Watching terrible stories of
    animals,
Ministers at 10 Downing
    Street
Do nothing except talk
About rotten political affairs.

It makes me sick to hear
That in this country, every
    week
Animals are being
    slaughtered just
For someone to prance
    about and speak
About their new fur coat. I'd
    love to
Tear the coat from off their
    backs.

And stamp on it with muddy
    shoes.
Oh it makes me sick, it really
    does.
Animals have such a rotten
    life
And no one does anything
    about it.
Killing young animals is the
    worst thing
You can do in your life.

If children need support in
writing about their feelings,
give them a starter line to work
from. These can be used to
begin each line, alternate lines,
or at the beginning of each
verse.

Possible starter lines
include:
• I felt/feel happy/sad/angry/
cross/upset when...;

• I care about...;
• I remember...;
• I get embarrassed when...;
• When I'm happy I...;
• When I'm cross I...;
• When I see....

# 2. Friends and enemies

### Age range
Six and upwards.

### Group size
The whole class, pairs and
small groups.

### What you need
Poems on friends and
friendship.

### What to do
Children's friendships often
change from day to day. It is
not unusual to hear a six-year-
old say, 'She's not my friend
any more – I hate her' about
someone she was good friends
with a mere half hour ago. But
the same children can come
back in from play close friends
again, the aggression gone.

Older children may have
difficulty sharing friends.
'We're not friends anymore,
she's playing with Tanya'. It is
as if one cannot be friendly or
play with more than one
person at the same time. Girls

often have more of a problem
with this than boys, who tend
to play in gangs or teams. But
these groups too can hurt and
exclude certain children. (See
'Picking Teams' by Allan
Ahlberg in *Please Mrs Butler*
[Puffin].) Once a friendship is
broken the children can be
unbelievably nasty to each
other, so it is important to
spend time on the friends/
enemies theme.

• Read 'Wrestling' by Kathleen
Fraser in Michael Rosen's
anthology *A World of Poetry*
(Kingfisher Books). This is
typical of the way children
make, break and remake
friendships. Discuss the poem
with the children. Ask them
what it is that breaks up their
friendships, and encourage
them to talk about these
reasons and look at their
validity.

• Read 'Moving In' by Marisa
Horsford, from Michael Rosen's
*A World of Poetry* (Kingfisher
Books). Do the children feel it
reflects how they feel in a new
situation, perhaps when
moving into the area, or
transferring from one school to
another?

• Ask each pair or small group
of children to draw the open
hand of friendship and the
clenched fist of aggression and
write in them appropriate
words and phrases. Then they
can use the words to write a
poem on either theme, or one
that deals with both.

• Useful poems on the theme
of friends and enemies include
'When you meet your friend'
and 'With clothes', from Morag
Styles's anthology *I Like That
Stuff* (Cambridge University
Press); 'Partners' by Judith
Nicholls in *Midnight Forest*
(Faber and Faber); 'It is a
Puzzle' by Allan Ahlberg in
*Please Mrs Butler* (Puffin).

## Further activity

Ask the children to write a poem in dialogue form on the subject of friends and enemies. They could use Kathleen Fraser's poem 'Wrestling' (see above) and translate that into a dialogue poem.

# 3. Bullying

## Age range

Six and upwards.

## Group size

The whole class, small groups and pairs.

## What you need

Poems on bullying.

## What to do

There are various poems on the topic of bullying. Good ones include 'Get off this estate' by Carl Sandberg, 'I've got an apple ready' by John Walsh and 'Canal lock in winter' by Gregory Harrison, all from Wes Magee's *All the Day Through* (Evans).

Read some appropriate poems to the children. Tell them that you want them to think about bullying, and to address the following questions in their groups.
• Have they experienced bullying?
• Was it done to them?
• Did they see someone being bullied?
• How did they feel?
• What did they do?

Ask the children to create a poem about bullying in their groups or pairs. Give them ten minutes to start writing the poem, and then ask them to read to the class what they have written so far. The other children can then suggest

possible angles to develop, and you can give them some more time to work on the poem.

Bring the children back together to hear the finished poems.

## Further activities

Talk with the children about why they think some people become bullies, and how they can deal with them. Ask them to devise slogans stating how to win against bullies. Display the children's poems about bullying against a playground or street setting, with the slogans written boldly on banners.

# 4. Know-alls

## Age range

Eight and upwards.

## Group size

The whole class.

## What you need

Copies of 'Dad and the Cat and the Tree' by Kit Wright, in *Rabbiting On* (Puffin) and 'I Hate Know Alls' by Max Fatchen in *Songs for my Dog and Other People* (Puffin).

## What to do

Ask the children what they think makes a person a 'know-all'. Explore what they think the

expression means, but neither agree nor disagree.

Read the poems to the children and discuss the contents. What do they think about Dad in 'Dad and the Cat and the Tree', and what he gets up to? What would have happened in the end if Dad had left the cat where it was? Was there a problem other than the cat up the tree? Do they know people like that? Do they tend to be like that sometimes? What effect does it have on others?

Talk about the advice others give. Is it always right to follow it blindly, or should we consider the arguments for and against? Alternatively, should we ignore other people's advice and go blithely on with what we are doing?

Discuss 'I Hate Know Alls' in a similar way.

## Further activity

Prepare Kit Wright's poem for performance, perhaps at an assembly. Make three groups, perhaps with girls to read the part of the mother, boys to read the father and a mixed group as narrator. You may like to have a group of actors to mime the parts while the poem is read.

## 5. The best things are free

### Age range
Eight and upwards.

### Group size
Small groups, pairs and individuals.

### What you need
A copy of 'Leisure' by W.H. Davies in *The Book of a Thousand Poems* (Unwin Hyman).

### What to do
Read 'Leisure' by W.H. Davies, which begins:

> What is this life if, full of care,
> We have no time to stand and stare....

In the world today there is so much concern for possessions. The children's attention needs to be drawn to the fact that some of the most beautiful things in the world are free for us to enjoy, to gaze upon and to wonder at.

Ask the children to write down ten beautiful or interesting things that cost nothing more than time. Having listed the things, the children should decide on a suitable form for their poem – it may be a haiku, a cinquain, a mini-poem, an acrostic, a chorus poem or one of the other forms mentioned in Chapter 8.

## Art
With proper planning, art and poetry can be used to complement each other. Art should not be used to lessen the power of poetry, but rather to provide an additional medium through which a response to a poem can be expressed.

Art can be created by individuals, pairs, groups or a whole class, and can range in size from a tiny, exquisite drawing to a large wall frieze.

Representing a poem by painting, drawing or craft work can add considerably to children's understanding of the piece. Because they have constantly to refer back to the poem for detail, children come to know it in greater depth. Allow the children to use their pictures to express what *they* see in the poem, rather than imposing your own view of it.

Story poems – ballads, folk songs, epic poems, narrative and descriptive poems – are all good sources of inspiration for artwork. The following ideas give some suggestions for combining art with poetry:
• Spontaneous illustrations, especially by young children, will stimulate language. The children (or a scribe) can write down the phrases that a picture brings to mind and create a poem from them.
• Present poems in the style of an illustrated manuscript, with attractive borders and a decorated first letter.
• Vary the scale from large to small, by representing a large picture in a tight poetic form or using a miniature as the spark for a narrative poem.
• Use separate illustrations to represent parts of a poem, and make a wall display or frieze to link them together and lead the viewer through the events in a narrative or epic poem.
• Take a poem like 'The Quangle Wangle's Hat' by Edward Lear and create a collage or models of the

colourful creatures that inhabit the poem.

Provide a wide range of tools and media for the children to use. Encourage them to draw with charcoal, chalk and pastels as well as pencils and pens, and to paint with powder colours and ready-mixed paint of different consistencies. The children could experiment with different sorts of collage, with sculpture and with printing.

Do not try to create art from every narrative or descriptive poem. The media of paint, pencil or collage should not be overused or they will become tedious. Be selective and vary the outcomes; sometimes read a poem for its own sake, just to enjoy it.

# 1. Colour me red

## Age range
Five to six as a class activity; seven and upwards in groups.

## Group size
The whole class, small groups, pairs and individuals.

## What you need
A display of items and poems about things of the same colour, such as red; a large sheet of paper and red felt-tipped pen, a collection of 'colour' poems, pictures of red things from magazines.

## What to do
Red is the colour suggested here, but any colour can be used for a similar range of activities.
• With the children, set up a display of red objects.
• Encourage them to paint pictures in tones of red, starting with white and then adding red paint drop by drop. If they are using powder paint, they should mix it first with water. Red is a strong colour, and only the merest drop is needed to deepen the tone (never start with red and try to lighten the tone, you'll be there all day trying).

• The children could cut out pictures of red things from magazines, and cut or tear them into pieces, making a mosaic picture.
• Put up reproductions of paintings in which red is dominant, such as Monet's painting 'The Poppy Field'. Use photographs of a strong red sunrise or sunset.
• Read poems about red things with the children, and talk about things that are always red and things that change to red as they ripen. How does the colour red make the children feel?
• Remind the children of the old saying 'Red sky at night...'. Can they think of any other sayings involving colours?
• Make a list of all the words that describe red and its tones.
• Write similes and metaphors for the colour red on a large sheet of paper with a large red pen. Use a recurring phrase, such as 'Red is like...' or 'Red is...'.
• Ask the children what red reminds them of, and ask them to place it in a context; for example, 'Red is a tomato growing by the wall'. Write their sentences on the paper or chalkboard. Tap out the rhythm of each line and, by redrafting, create lines of similar length. Discuss the order of the lines and write them on a large sheet of paper to create a class poem. If the children work in groups, each child can devise two lines and then the group can work together to create a poem.
• Look at a range of poems about colour with the children. Suitable poems could include 'Old Tom Tomato' by Geoffrey Lapage in *Bedtime Rhymes*

(Ladybird), 'Red' by Lilian Moore, 'Blue is a Lake' and 'The Colours Live' by Mary O'Neil, 'Colours' by Jean Kenward and 'The Paint Box' by E.V. Rieu from *The First Lick of the Lolly*, chosen by Moira Andrew (Macmillan), 'A Slash of Blue' by Emily Dickinson from *A World of Poetry*, selected by Michael Rosen (Kingfisher Books).

# 2. Footprints

### Age range
Six to nine.

### Group size
Individuals and small groups.

### What you need
Newspapers, a flat washing-up sponge (the kind that goes hard when dry), powder paint mixed with water, a bowl of clean water, a towel, a large sheet of cheap white paper, a long strip of lining paper, two chairs.

### What to do
Soak the sponge in the paint, and place it on a pile of newspaper to the right of a chair. Position the sheet of white paper in front of the chair, and a bowl of warm water and a towel on the other side.

The children should take it in turns to sit on the chair, press their feet on the sponge, twist to the front and press their feet on to the paper to make footprints, then twist to the other side to rinse off the paint. Swiftly move the footprints before they get splashed!

If you want to make a trail, place a chair at each end of a long strip of lining paper, with the chair legs on top of the paper to keep it flat. The children should press their feet on the sponge at one end and then walk along the strip to the washing bowl by the chair at the other end.

Read the chapter in *Winnie the Pooh* by A.A. Milne (Methuen), where Pooh and Piglet go Woozle hunting. How would the children have felt if they had suddenly come across tracks in the way that Pooh and Piglet did? Would they be anxious or pleased to meet someone?

Talk with the children about tracks and footprints in the mud and the snow, and stress also the importance of not going tracking on their own, or going anywhere without first asking their parents or carers if they may.

Use the feelings generated by this discussion to create a poem. If it is a tense poem, very short lines carry the right kind of message. If it is happy-go-lucky or dreamy, longer lines help to create the mood. Mount the poems alone or beside some of the tracks.

### Further activity
Ask the children to write a short poem about the way the paint felt as they pressed their feet on the sponge, or how they felt when they saw their footprints. Haiku, mini-poems and cinquains all lend themselves to this kind of poetry.

in verse to attract the attention of visitors.

• Ask pairs or groups to design a new drink and write a rhyming slogan for it that is easy to remember and can be said without stumbling.

• Ask the children to write a rhyming couplet, with a maximum of twenty words, for a new flavour of potato crisps.

• Together, devise a chant for your class telling the world that it is the best class ever.

• Encourage the children to write rhyming advertisements for the local shop, bringing in the shopkeeper's name, saying something about him or her and the delights (or otherwise) of the shop itself. They should use colourful descriptive words that employ all the senses, pulling the reader into the heart of the shop's atmosphere.

## 2. Selling labels

### Age range
Seven and upwards.

### Group size
Small groups and pairs.

### What you need
Labels from tinned and packaged goods.

### What to do
The idea behind these poems is that the words are already there, so the children can concentrate on the rhythm of the lines.

Ask the children to soak the labels off tins or cut labels from packaged goods and bring three or four to school. The words on the labels or packages should then be copied out, cut up and sorted into some kind of rhythm. Unnecessary words can be thrown away and apposite ones added to enhance the pattern.

## 3. Plead and persuade

### Age range
Nine and upwards.

### Group size
Small groups, pairs and individuals.

### What you need
No special requirements.

### What to do
How often have the children had to take on a pleading role in an attempt to persuade their parents to allow them to do something or to explain away something they have done?

Encourage them to talk about it and explore the language they used.

Read Michael Rosen's 'If you don't put your shoes on before I count fifteen' and 'I'm the youngest in our house' in *You Can't Catch Me* (Puffin).

Tell the children to think of something they would really like to do and to write a poem trying to persuade their parents to let them do it. They should try to make it humorous and present it attractively, so as to put their parents into a happy and relaxed frame of mind before coming to the plea.

Try a similar exercise in pairs, with one partner as the child and the other as the parent. They should take it in turns to write a line or a couplet in response to each other. Start them off with a few lines like these:

'Mu – um...'
'What is it, child?'
'About the party...'

'Where have you been?
Why are you late?'
'I'm sorry Mum
But by the gate
Was...'

### Further activities
• Individually, the children could write a begging letter as a poem:

My very dear Mum,
I'm just writing to say
You know when I asked you
The other day....

• The children could take the viewpoint of a well-known character from fiction or a famous contemporary or historical person, and think of an action they might have undertaken that was less than satisfactory. In character, they should write a poem about what happened and try to explain away the outcome.

# 4. Newspapers

### Age range
Ten and upwards.

### Group size
Small groups and pairs.

### What you need
A range of newspapers.

### What to do
Ask each child to bring to school a copy of yesterday's newspaper. The children should then compare the make-up of the papers, looking at the pages for news, sport, features, fashion and so on. What can they find out about the readership? What gives them clues?

Take the lead article and see how it is handled in different papers. Choose a piece of news, extrapolate the main idea and see how different papers present it for their readers.

Ask the children to choose a theme from the papers and write a poem about it. There may be a telling cartoon which focuses on an item of news. The children can choose to write a serious poem or a jokey one about their chosen theme.

### Further activities
• Choose an odd or quirky item from a newspaper and ask the children to write a limerick or clerihew about it.
• Ask the children to select an advertisement and write a new slogan for it.
• The children could try to devise a crossword using rhyming words.
• Ask them to make up an acrostic using the word 'news', the name of the paper or a person or feature in it.

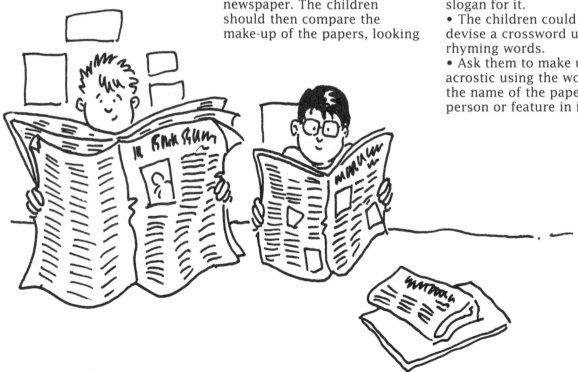

# CHAPTER 10

# Parading poetry

How we teach poetry determines how it is received. We need to create an atmosphere where poetry can be shared and enjoyed, but we also need to be aware that children's reaction to poetry is strongly affected by attitudes at home. Therefore, we need to present poetry to the parents, so that it is seen by them as relevant, worthwhile and a profitable activity for children to be involved in. We need to share with parents what children gain from poetry in terms that they see as valid, while also putting across the value of poetry for its own sake.

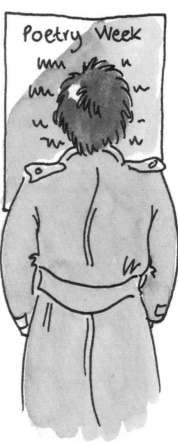

# BACKGROUND

One of the ways we come to like something and improve our competence at it is by knowing that others enjoy what we have achieved. Because of the positive feedback we gain from the response of others we feel good about what we have done. This feedback increases our self-confidence which engenders greater effort and gives us the willingness to carry on.

This chapter looks at ways of sharing poetry with others while developing a range of other skills.

## Audience

Children need an audience for their writing; their hard work deserves better than being condemned to lie inside the covers of an exercise book, or worse, consigned to the waste-paper basket. Teachers have a responsibility to seek out a range of audiences so that children have regular opportunities to share their writing with others.

Poetry tends to be a private activity, and some poems should always remain private, but the rest, where appropriate, should be shared. By sharing we gain feedback about our own competence and receive suggestions for improvements.

The main purpose of an audience is feedback, whether from the children's peers, their teachers, the rest of the school, the head, parents or the wider community. It can take the form of reading what children have written, congratulating them on their efforts, commenting constructively, attending a performance, clapping after a piece has been read, reviewing performances in the press and buying school publications.

Children need to realise that they, too, are an audience, not just for others but also for themselves.

As children's competence grows so should their audience and their opportunities to write for that audience. Their poetry should be considered important enough to be shared with real readers, and published so that it can be read and borrowed. If they see that their work is valued, children are more likely to take care with the preparation and presentation of their work.

Feedback from an audience is generally beneficial for writers, but not always. When children first begin to write, they are not concerned with what other people think, they are proud of their efforts. If the audience they face is not constructive, and misunderstands what they are trying to do, their confidence gradually wanes and they may even cease to write at all.

Writing must not be shared too soon. If someone intrudes before the piece is set in the writer's mind, if the reader ignores the writer's intention and overshadows it with concern for the quality of the writing in the first draft, so damning his efforts while still at embryo stage, the writer may well give up trying. Early audiences must not say too much, too soon. They must be receptive to what the writer is trying to do.

## Being your own audience

Vocal children, who have no inhibitions about speaking up or performing in front of others, can often find writing difficult, because they miss the audience, being able to look into the eyes of others and get instant feedback from their response.

Encourage these children to be their own audience, to sit quietly and read aloud to themselves their own writing, seeing it as a preparation for performance. These children need to write more, not less, not in longer sessions but in very short ones two or three times a day, two or three lines at a time, gradually building up to longer sessions. They need teacher time to lead them on, challenging them to write a little more each day and then giving them the chance to 'perform' the writing they have already achieved. Once audience and purpose are linked, these children are able to push forward.

There are innumerable ways of presenting poetry, of parading it in front of others. In this chapter we are looking at ways of reaching audiences, of sharing poetry with them and showing them that poetry covers a range of subjects and emotions, that it has a place in our society and that society is the richer for it.

# ACTIVITIES

## 1. Poetry board

### Age range
All ages.

### Group size
The whole class.

### What you need
Wall space, hessian, coloured card, basic mounts, steel pins.

### What to do
Make an attractive permanent area in the classroom for a wall display of poetry. Cover the area with hessian and frame or edge it neatly. Have a supply of lill pins available, and a range of basic mounts.

Give the children the freedom to put up their own poetry or poetry they have enjoyed, provided that it is well-presented.

Alternatively, all work can be put up at first and then the class can select which work remains up, which needs improving and so on. A poem which is to be worked on can be put up again later in the week.

At the beginning of each week have a short session when the children tidy up and decide which pieces of poetry on the poetry board should stay and which should come down to prevent the board becoming cluttered.

If the poetry board is used in this way, it becomes a focal point for the children's poetry and for discussion. Because it is purposefully used, it never becomes unnoticed. It maintains its viability and purpose within the classroom.

## 2. Poetry weeks

### Age range
All ages.

### Group size
Whole school involvement in a variety of groupings on a variety of levels.

### What you need
Support from colleagues, time for planning.

### What to do
Before you start to initiate a poetry week, think through the idea yourself and make a rough plan. Once you have done this discuss the idea with colleagues to make sure that you have some support; you cannot manage without it.

Discuss with the head an outline of what could take place and what you have in mind. Get together a small team and plan the week in detail. If you want to have a visiting poet, your first task must be to book one – they are busy people, and may have a full diary for as much as a year ahead. Go through your Regional Arts Council, who should have a list of poets who are willing to visit schools, and they may be persuaded to contribute towards the fees.

Once you have prepared this basic groundwork and fixed a date for the poetry week you can get on with the rest of the planning. Set out a schedule for tasks to be done and discuss the programme details with the staff. Make sure that everyone knows what is going on and ask for volunteers to take over the running of

particular events. Your task is to co-ordinate the week as a whole and to troubleshoot where necessary.

Ask a team of older children to set out the programme on a word processor and photocopy enough programmes so that each child is able to have one.

Send invitations and programmes to your governors, school inspector, the English inspector, chief inspector, county councillors, chairperson of the County Education Committee, the local HMI, your local MP and the mayor. This is a real opportunity to sell your school, to let the community know what is going on and the high standards you are achieving.

Ideas for a poetry week could include the following:
• 'Time for poetry' sessions – see Activity 5 on page 167.
• Hold verse speaking competitions for individuals, pairs, groups or whole classes.

• Put up a display of poems illustrated and written out by the children.
• Have poetry and other competitions for different age groups. Select from:
– free choice of topic and form;
– set form but free choice of topic (for example a limerick);
– free choice of form but set topic (for example, ripples);
– both topic and form set (for example a haiku on winter, an acrostic on a given word);
– a jingle for a product, real or imagined;
– a design for a poster to advertise the poetry week;
– a design for a poster to recommend a poetry book;
– a review of a poetry book;
– a short biography of a favourite poet;
– a song, with music and/or rhythm backing;
– a rap;
– a poem about a photograph (preferably their own).
– a poem and design for a Christmas card (see photocopiable page 186).

Do not have more than two competitions for any one age group.
• Invite a visiting poet to run workshops and judge competitions.

• Invite poetry groups – people who present published poetry to children and display a range of current books.
• Run a poetry bookshop – arrange with your local bookshop or county bookseller to set up a display of poetry books for parents and children to purchase. The discount could buy some more poetry books for your school!
• Have dramatic presentations.
• Ask a class or group to do some choral speaking.
• Hold a poetry evening to end the week, which could include poetry presentations to music, movement, the best from the week's events, displays of the competition entries – make it a celebration of poetry, a true culmination of the week's work.

Invite each special guest to donate a prize for one of the competitions. Write to National Book Week to obtain bookmarks and badges so that each child who enters a competition receives something.

Keep the rehearsals for the poetry evening to a minimum so that freshness is not lost and the excitement and anticipation replaced by boredom.

The emphasis on poetry in the weeks leading up to the poetry week, and its culmination in a poetry evening, will make it a week to be remembered. It will also lift the status of poetry in the eyes of the pupils and the community.

## 3. Poetry trolleys

### Age range
Five and upwards.

### Group size
The whole class and individuals.

### What you need
A growing collection of poetry books, a trolley.

### What to do
Collect all the poetry books in the school and take a good look at them. Put to one side all the damaged ones that can be mended and, separately, those beyond repair. These latter can be cut up, mounted and laminated for use in displays, as poetry work cards, or put in anthologies.

Sort the remaining books into two or four levels, for example, lower infants, upper infants, lower juniors, upper juniors. Some books will cover a range of ages. If you are lucky enough to have more than one copy, you can place them separately, otherwise put each book where it will be most used. In an ideal world there would be at least two copies of each book on a poetry trolley or in a box.

Once you know what resources you have, you can make a catalogue card for each book listing its details and where it is sited (another class may have borrowed it) and file them. I like to do this alphabetically, but under headings similar to those used in the bibliography on page 171.

Put your collection on a trolley which can be wheeled from class to class. A trolley, rather than a box, allows books to be displayed and encourages browsing. When browsing, children are selecting, rejecting, sharing and discussing their likes and dislikes in terms of poets, poems, topics and the language used. This all adds to their understanding of poetry.

The ultimate aim, of course, is to have a poetry collection for each classroom. Unfortunately this is not often possible.

Armed with a booklist, perhaps taken from the bibliography or one of the recommended lists, gradually build up your poetry collection.

You may be able to have a 'Buy a book for school' stall. Send a note to parents explaining clearly why you need poetry books, your desperate shortage (put what you have on show so they know you are not fooling), and place a 'Presented to... by...' label inside any that they buy. Make sure there are a number of less expensive books on sale; there are many slim volumes that cost less than a drink in a pub these days.

Systematically buy from your list the books you need, crossing them off as you order them. Make a card for each one that comes in and add it to your catalogue file. You need to keep your records and your list up to date so that you can refer to it when you have the opportunity to order and methodically fill the gaps on your poetry bookshelves.

# 4. Assembly

### Age range
Five and upwards.

### Group size
The whole school.

### What you need
No special requirements.

### What to do
Hold poetry assemblies in which a member of staff reads a favourite poem to the rest of the school. Each poem should be introduced with a short talk on why the individual likes it and why he or she chose to read it that day. It may take time for all the staff to join in, but there's nothing like pupil blackmail when a class sees that their teacher is one of the few who has not contributed!

Invite the children to form groups of up to eight so that they can share their favourite poems in a similar way. Parents and governors, non-teaching staff, senior citizens, pupils from the local secondary school, local community workers and residents may also be willing to take a session, either alone or in groups. Try to reach across different cultures, religions, positions and ages.

This kind of sharing serves to bring to the children the knowledge that poetry is not just for schools, visiting poets and media presentations. There is something in poetry for everyone.

# 5. Time for poetry

### Age range
Five and upwards.

### Group size
The whole school or class.

### What you need
Poems and people.

### What to do
There are two kinds of 'time for poetry' sessions, informal and formal. Each is concerned with bringing poetry to children.

#### Informal sessions
The length of an informal session should be between 20 and 30 minutes for infants and up to 45 minutes for juniors. The number of poems each class brings to the session will depend on the number of classes in the school, but a limit of six poems per class is reasonable. It is as well to have a couple in reserve yourself in case someone is unavailable at the last minute or there is extra time to fill.

Choose a theme for your session. The poems could be funny, sad, about nature, the weather, home, family, flowers, animals, the list is endless. Get together with other members of staff to make a cohesive programme.

In their own classrooms, the children should prepare possible poems, suggesting and reading them to see if they fit the theme. The poems can be published poems or ones they have written themselves, and they may be performed solo, in pairs, or in small groups.

On the day of the session bring the children into the hall and sit them in a horseshoe shape, or fanning out from a corner, facing a different way from assembly. You may like to have a presenter who

introduces the poems and acts as the link person, or you may prefer each child to introduce their own and say why they chose that particular poem. They should then say or read the poems they want to share.

### Formal sessions

A formal session is similar to an informal one, but each class is given a slot of time to fill with a poetry presentation. It can be a choral speaking of, for example, "Twas the night before Christmas' or 'The Pied Piper', or it can be a group, pair or solo performance of poems the children have

written on a specific topic, with their own poems intermingled with published ones. Keep props and costumes to a minimum, since the idea is for the poems to speak for themselves through the mouths of the pupils.

# 6. Publishing poetry

### Age range
Five and upwards.

### Group size
Any, as appropriate.

### What you need
Mounting materials, book-making materials, a word processor.

### What to do
Poems can be published in a number of different ways: as part of a display, in school magazines and county

publications, in the local press, through poetry competitions and in booklets.

Even though someone may have scribed for them, there is no reason why poems by five-year-olds should not go into booklets. Find a willing parent to type them out or an older child to print the poems using a word processor. Let the younger child stand alongside the 'secretary' and watch the poem take shape on the page.

Older children can use their skills in layout, handwriting, calligraphy and illustration to present pages that can be mounted and sewn into a book.

Make A5-size booklets by folding A4 sheets in half and stitching or stapling them between attractive covers. Poems can be typed and the pages adorned with drawings done by the children. These books could be used for collections of poems written by one child or for group editions. The focus could be on one subject or a particular poetic form. A narrative poem could fill a booklet of its own.

Collections of word puzzles, riddles and jokes make humorous little books, and anthologies can also be

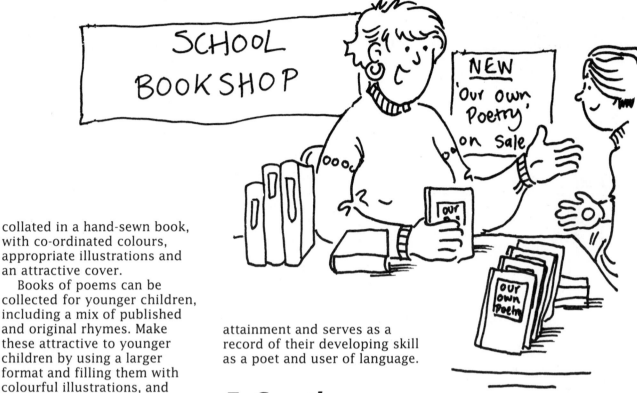

collated in a hand-sewn book, with co-ordinated colours, appropriate illustrations and an attractive cover.

Books of poems can be collected for younger children, including a mix of published and original rhymes. Make these attractive to younger children by using a larger format and filling them with colourful illustrations, and using revelation and pop-up techniques.

Put the booklets and collections on sale within the school and at various events which bring the community into the school.

Other avenues we may not automatically think of as ways of publishing poetry are media messages like posters, advertisements and rules. Put up the children's jokes, puns, and word puzzles around the school for everyone to read as they pass by.

Publishing is important for all children, and every child deserves to see his or her work in print. It shows children where they are (or were) at a particular time, reminding them of the path they trod to reach this result. It is also a sign to others of their

attainment and serves as a record of their developing skill as a poet and user of language.

## 7. Creating a class anthology

### Age range
Six and upwards.

### Group size
Individuals.

### What you need
Poems, paper, pens, crayons, a file (preferably a ring binder).

### What to do
Show the children your own anthology and talk about the different kinds of poems it contains. Say why you wanted to include them.

As the children learn poems and rhymes, suggest that they might want to include them in a class anthology. Invite the children to write out poems, illustrating them beautifully, and then let them mount them and put them in the file. Younger children may need help with this, but each child should have at least one poem in the class anthology.

Other poems that the children have written for topics or that have been displayed or written for other purposes can each be transferred straight to the anthology.

There are a number of different ways of collating the poems. One way is to have sections within the anthology and to discuss with the children where it is appropriate to place the poem. Another way is to make thematic anthologies for aspects of a subject or topic.

The anthologies become a useful addition to your class library in succeeding years. No two years' anthologies will be the same. Different kinds of poetry appeal to children of the same age and similar background experiences.

# 8. Poets at work

### Age range
Eight and upwards.

### Group size
The whole class and individuals.

### What you need
Willing poets to supply some drafts of a poem and the finished copy, transparencies of the draft.

### What to do
Write to a couple of poets and ask if they would be willing to share with your class the way one of their poems developed. Children need to see that real poets don't get it right first time, that they too cross out and make additions as they redraft their work.

They need to supply you with the first draft, later drafts and the published version of one of their poems. Show the first draft to the children and discuss any changes that might be made. Show the next draft, and compare the changes they suggested with the ones the poet made. Were the changes the same? Why do they think that the poet made certain changes? For what purpose or effect? Compare the original with the final version. What has happened to the poem?

Ask the children to write a poem in a similar form and work through it following the ideas evoked by the poet.

You may even be able to find a poet who is willing to come into your classroom and explain his or her redrafting technique.

### Further activity
Display the children's finished poems alongside the work of the poets. Include in the display the drafts showing the process the poets went through, and some of the children's redrafting as well. Make a notice to explain the purpose of the altered copies.

# CHAPTER 11

## Bibliography

The books listed here are divided into two sections – books for teachers and books for children. The section for teachers also contains details of other useful resources in the form of magazines, journals, photograph collections and ideas to help enhance the presentation of poems.

The children's books are sorted into broad categories for easy reference. The lists provide a starting point to help you select suitable books for your class, but many journals and magazines regularly publish reviews of the latest books, and it is worth reading these to keep up with what is available.

# Books for teachers

## Books about children and their writing

Beard, R. (1984) *Children's Writing in the Primary School*, Hodder and Stoughton.

Britton, J. (1972) *Language and Learning*, Penguin.

Graves, D. (1983) *Writing: Teachers and Children at Work*, Heinemann Educational.

Holdaway, D. (1979) *The Foundations of Literacy*, Ashton Scholastic.

Raban, B. (Ed.) (1985) *Practical Ways to Teach Writing*, Ward Lock Educational.

Rosen, C. and Rosen, H. (1973) *The Language of Primary School Children*, Penguin.

## Books to help you teach poetry

Andrew, M. (1989) *Language in Colour*, Belair Publications.

Balaam, J. and Merrick, B. (1987) *Exploring Poetry :5–8*, National Association for the Teaching of English.

Benton, M.G. and Benton, P. (1979–1982) *Watchwords One, Two* and *Three*, Hodder and Stoughton.

Benton, M.G., Benton, P., Benton, S. and Fox, G. (1985–1986) *Beginnings* Series: *Names, Noah, Witches, Halloween and Guy Fawkes*, Hodder and Stoughton.

Brownjohn, S. (1980) *Does it have to Rhyme?*, Hodder and Stoughton.

Brownjohn, S. (1982) *What Rhymes with Secret?*, Hodder and Stoughton.

Brownjohn, S. and Brownjohn, A. (1985) *Meet and Write* (three books), Hodder and Stoughton.

Brownjohn, S. and Whitaker, J. (1985) *More Word Games*, Hodder and Stoughton.

Brownjohn, S. and Whitaker, J. (1985) *Word Games*, Hodder and Stoughton.

Calthrop, K. and Ede, J. (1984) *Not 'Daffodils' Again! Teaching Poetry 9–13*, Longman.

Corbett, P. and Moses, B. (1986) *Catapults and Kingfishers*, Oxford University Press.

Elliott-Kemp, H. (1982) *Developing Poetic Writing in the Middle Years*, Sheffield City Polytechnic Library.

Hall, L. (1989) *Poetry for Life*, Cassell.

Hughes, T. (1969) *Poetry in the Making*, Faber and Faber.

Opie, I. and Opie, P. (1959) *The Lore and Language of Schoolchildren*, Oxford University Press/Granada.

Reeves, J. (1981) *How to Write Poems for Children*, Heinemann.

Reeves, J. (1958) *Teaching Poetry*, Heinemann.

Reeves, J. (1979) *Understanding Poetry*, Heinemann Educational.

Rosen, M. (1989) *Did I Hear You Write*, Andre Deutsch.

Scannell, V. (1982) *How to Enjoy Poetry*, Piatkus.

## Journals and magazines

*Books for Keeps*, School Bookshop Association, 6 Brightfield Road, London SE12 8QF; six issues per year.

*Children's Literature in Education*, details from Mrs B. Collinge, 2 Sunwine Place, Exmouth, Devon; four issues per year.

*Creative Language* (used to be called *Schools Poetry Review*) edited by David Orme; three issues per year, published by Stanley Thornes.

*The School Librarian*, School Library Association, Liden Library, Barrington Close, Liden, Swindon SN6 6HF; four issues per year.

*Signal*, edited by Nancy Chambers, published by The Thimble Press, Lockwood, Station Road, South Woodchester, Stroud, Glos GL5 5EQ; three issues per year.

*The Times Educational Supplement* has three children's books editions every year as well as weekly reviews.

*The Use of English*, subscription details from Scottish Academic Press, 3 Montgomery Street, Edinburgh EH7 5JX; three issues per year.

## Books containing reviews and resources

Bennett, J. and Chambers, A. *Poetry for Children*, A Signal Bookguide, Thimble Press.

Morris, H. (1985) *The New Where's That Poem*, Blackwell.

Rowe, A. (1989) *101 Good Poetry Books*, Reading and Language Information Centre, University of Reading.

Styles, M. and Triggs, P. (1988) *Poetry 0–16*, Books for Keeps.

## Other resources

*Borders, Layouts and Designs* by Sue Bastian – copyright-free illustrations and borders, ideal for layout and presentation work. Alpha Visuals, 18 Dove Close, Thorley Park, Bishops Stortford, Herts.

Drake Educational *Graph-Ed*, a series of motifs, copyright-free, to enhance the layout of children's written work, especially poetry. Twelve titles covering different curriculum topics. St Fagan's Road, Fairwater, Cardiff CF5 3AE.

Philip Green Educational supplies superb photographs in poetry and poster packs, a useful stimulus for children's poetry writing. 112a Alcester Road, Studley, Warks B80 7NR.

*Poets in Schools* – information from The Education Department, The Poetry Society, 21 Earls Court Square, London SW5 9DE.

# Books for children

## Poems for the very young

Bennett, J. (1980) *Roger was a Razor Fish*, Bodley Head/ Hippo.

Blake, Q. (1980) *Mister Magnolia*, Cape/Armada Picture Lions.

Blake, Q. (1983) *Quentin Blake's Nursery Rhyme Book*, Cape/ Armada Picture Lions.

Foster, J.L. (1985) *A Very First Poetry Book*, Oxford University Press.

Hughes, S. (1988) *Out and About*, Walker Books.

Ireson, B. (1984) *Rhyme Time*, Beaver Books.

Ireson, B. (1970) *The Young Puffin Book of Verse*, Puffin.

Matterson, E. (1969) *This Little Puffin*, Puffin.

Opie, I. and Opie, P. (1970) *The Puffin Book of Nursery Rhymes*, Puffin.

Oxenbury, H. (1986) *The Helen Oxenbury Nursery Rhyme Book*, Heinemann.

Samson, C. (1974–1975) *Speech Rhymes, Acting Rhymes* and *Counting Rhymes*, A & C Black.

## Old favourites (anthologies and collections)

Blishen, E. (Ed.) (1963) *Oxford Book of Poetry for Children*, Oxford University Press.

Graham, E. (Ed.) (1969) *A Puffin Book of Verse*, Puffin.

Macbain, J.M. (Ed.) (1986) *Book of 1000 Poems*, Bell and Hyman.

Opie, I. and Opie, P. (1973) *The Oxford Book of Children's Verse*, Oxford University Press.

Read, H. (1957) *This Way Delight*, Faber Fanfare.

Untermeyer, L. (Ed.) (1961) *The Golden Treasury of Poetry*, Collins.

## Modern ones (anthologies and collections)

Andrew, M. (Ed.) (1988) *My Blue Poetry Book*, Macmillan Education.

Andrew, M. (Ed.) (1988) *My Red Poetry Book*, Macmillan Education.

Andrew, M. (Ed.) (1988) *My Violet Poetry Book*, Macmillan Education.

Andrew, M. (Ed.) (1988) *Open the Door to Poetry: Teacher's Guide*, Macmillan Education.

Andrew, M. (Ed.) (1986) *Poetry 1: The First Lick of the Lolly*, Macmillan Education.

Andrew, M. (Ed.) (1986) *Poetry 2: Marbles in my Pocket*, Macmillan Education.

Andrew, M. (Ed.) (1987) *Poetry 3: Go and Open the Door*, Macmillan Education.

Andrew, M. (Ed.) (1987) *Poetry 4: The Unicorn and Lions*, Macmillan Education.

Benton, M.G. and Benton, P. (Ed.) (1979–1982) *Watchwords*, Books One, Two and Three, Hodder and Stoughton.

Causley, C. (Ed.) (1978) *The Puffin Book of Salt Sea Verse*, Puffin.

Corrin, S. and Corrin S. (Ed.) (1982) *Once Upon a Rhyme*, Faber/Puffin.

Cribbins, B. (Ed.) (1988) *Along the Line*, Macdonald.

Foster, J.L. (Ed.) (1981–1989) *First, Second, Third, Fourth* and *Fifth Poetry Books*, Oxford University Press.

Kemp, G. (Ed.) (1980) *Ducks and Dragons*, Faber/Puffin.

McGough, R. (Ed.) (1985) *Strictly Private*, Puffin.

Magee, W. (1985) *Poetry One: Dragon's Smoke*, Basil Blackwell.

Magee, W. (1985) *Poetry Two: A Shooting Star*, Basil Blackwell.

Nicoll, H. (Ed.) (1984) *Poems for 7 Year Olds and Under*, Viking Kestrel/Puffin.

Thwaite, A. (1980) *All Sorts of Poems*, Magnet.

Watson, J. (1973) *The Armada Lion Book of Young Verse*, Armada Lions.

Wilson, R. (1987), *Out and About*, Viking Kestrel/Puffin.

Wright, K. (1985) *Poems for 9 Year Olds and Under*, Puffin.

## Singles collection (poems by one poet)

Ahlberg, A. (1984) *Please Mrs Butler*, Viking Kestrel/Puffin.

Belloc, H. (1974) *A Bad Child's Book of Beasts*, Duckworth.

Belloc, H. (1970) *Cautionary Tales for Children*, Duckworth.

Causley, C. (1979) *Figgie Hobbin*, Viking Kestrel/Puffin.

Cotton, J. and Sedgwick, F. (1990) *Hey*, Mary Glasgow.

Cotton, J. and Sedgwick, F. (1990) *The Biggest Riddle in the World*, Mary Glasgow.

Eliot, T.S. (1940) *Old Possum's Book of Practical Cats*, Faber and Faber.

Hughes, T. (1977) *Meet My Folks*, Puffin.

Mare, W. de la (1978) *Come Hither*, Viking Kestrel.

Mare, W. de la (1988) *Peacock Pie*, Faber and Faber.

McGough, R. (1983) *Sky in the Pie*, Viking Kestrel/Puffin.

Nicholls, J. (1985) *Magic Mirror*, Faber and Faber.

Nicholls, J. (1987) *Midnight Forest*, Faber and Faber.

Nicholls, J. (1988) *Popcorn Pie*, Mary Glasgow.

Nicholls, J. (Ed.) (1989) *What on Earth...?*, Faber and Faber.

Nicholls, J. (1988) *Word Spells*, Faber and Faber.

Reeves, J. (1973) *Complete Poems for Children*, Heinemann.

Rosen, M. (1974) *Mind Your Own Business*, Deutsch/Armada Lions.

Rosen, M. (1977) *Wouldn't You Like to Know*, Deutsch/Puffin.

Rosen, M. (1981) *You Can't Catch Me*, Deutsch/Puffin.

Silverstein, S. (1982) *A Light in the Attic*, Cape.

Silverstein, S. (1984) *Where the Sidewalk Ends*, Cape.

Wright, K. (1982) *Hot Dog*, Puffin.

Wright, K. (1978) *Rabbiting On*, Armada Lions.

## Thematic anthologies

Causley, C. (1974) *The Puffin Book of Magic Verse*, Kestrel/Puffin.

Causley, C. (1978) *The Puffin Book of Salt-sea Verse*, Kestrel/Puffin.

Causley, C. (1982) *The Sun, Dancing* (Christian Verse), Viking Kestrel/Puffin.

Davis, D. (1976) *A Single Star* (Christmas), Puffin.

Foster, J.L. (1986) *Spaceways*, Oxford University Press.

Magee, W. (1982) *All the Day Through*, Evans.

Magee, W. (1986) *A Calendar of Poems*, Bell and Hyman.

Magee, W. (1988) *A Christmas Stocking*, Cassell.

Rumble, A. (1987) *Shadow Dance* (poems of the night), Cassell.

## Anglo-Saxon and mediaeval poetry

Chaucer, G. (1970) *The Canterbury Tales*, (translated into modern rhyming verse by Nevill Coghill), Penguin Classics.

Crossley-Holland, K. (1982) *Beowulf*, Oxford University Press.

Grigson, G. (1975) *The Penguin Book of Ballads*, Penguin.

Serraillier, I. (1954) *Beowulf the Warrior*, Oxford University Press.

Serraillier, I. (1981) *The Challenge of the Green Knight*, Heinemann Educational.

## Humorous poems

Blakeley, P. (1978) *Nonsense Rhymes*, A & C Black.

Cole, W. (1970) *Beastly Boys and Ghastly Girls*, Methuen/Magnet.

Cole, W. (1975) *Oh, How Silly!*, Methuen/Magnet.

Cole, W. (1982) *Oh, Such Foolishness!*, Methuen/Magnet.

Cole, W. (1975) *Oh, That's Ridiculous!*, Methuen/Magnet.

Dahl, R. (1982) *Revolting Rhymes*, Cape/Picture Puffin.

Edgar, M. (1980) *The Lion and Albert*, Methuen.

Grigson, G. (Ed.) (1977) *The Faber Book of Epigrams and Epitaphs*, Faber and Faber.

Lear, E. (1988) *Book of Nonsense*, Hamlyn.

McGough, R. (1986) *The Kingfisher Book of Comic Verse*, Kingfisher.

Milligan, S. (1970) *Silly Verse for Kids*, Puffin.

Nash, O. (1981) *Custard and Company*, Puffin.

Peake, M. (1978) *Rhymes Without Reason*, Methuen.

Silcock, A. (1971) *Verse and Worse*, Faber and Faber.

Watson, J. (Ed.) (1981) *The Puffin Book of Funny Verse*, Puffin.

Webster, C. (1987) *Poetry through Humour and Horror*, Cassell.

Wilson, R. (1978) *The Beaver Book of Funny Verse*, Beaver.

Woodward, Z. and Woodward, I. (1983) *Poems for Fun*, Beaver.

## Children's own poems

Astley, N. (Ed.) (1987) *Bossy Parrot* (children's poems from the *Evening Chronicle* competition), Bloodaxe.

*Cadbury's Books of Children's Poetry* (annual since 1983), Beaver.

*Words on Water* (1987) (poems from the Young Observer National Children's Poetry Competition), Viking Kestrel/Puffin.

Worthy, W. (Ed.) (1970) *Mirror Poems* (by children six to twelve), Ginn.

*Young Words* (annual since 1959) (entries from the W.H. Smith Young Writers' Competition), Macmillan.

## Poems from other cultures

Agard, J. (1984) *I Din Do Nuttin* (West Indian), Bodley Head/Magnet.

Aardema, V. (1986) *Bringing the Rain to Kapiti Plain* (African), Macmillan.

Basho, M. (1970) *The Narrow Road to the Deep North* (Haiku), Penguin Classics.

Bownas, G. and Thwaite, A. (1970) *The Penguin Book of Japanese Verse*, Penguin.

Styles, M. (1984) *I Like That Stuff* (poems from many cultures), Cambridge University Press.

# AT CHARTS

## England and Wales

Use this chart to identify the English attainment targets covered by the activities in this book. The activity numbers in Chapter 9 are prefaced by initials which refer to the sections in this chapter.

**NB** The skills of reading, spelling and handwriting are practised and reinforced by various tasks, but are not taught specifically in this book.

| AT / Chapter | 1 Speaking and listening | 2 Reading | 3 Writing | 4 Spelling | 5 Handwriting |
|---|---|---|---|---|---|
| 1 | 1, 2, 3, 4, 5, 6, 7, 8, 9, 10, 11, 12 | 1, 3, 6, 11 | 3, 5, 6, 7, 8 | | |
| 2 | 2, 3, 6, 7, 8, 10, 11, 12 | 1, 4, 5, 6, 11 | | | 1 |
| 3 | 1, 2, 5, 6, 7, 8, 10, 11 12, 13, 15, 16, 17, 18 | 1, 3, 5, 7, 11, 12, 16 | 2, 3, 4, 5, 6, 7, 8, 9, 11, 13, 14, 15, 16, 17, 18 | | 9, 11, 16, 18 |
| 4 | 1, 2, 4, 5, 8, 10,11, 12 | 1, 2, 3, 5, 6, 8, 10, 11, 12 | 1, 5, 9, 11, 12 | 7, 11 | 6, 7, 10, |
| 5 | 2, 3, 5, 6, 7, 8, 9, 11, 12, 14, 15 | 1, 2, 3, 4, 9, 10, 11, 12, 13 | 3, 4, 6, 7, 8, 9, 10, 11, 12, 14, 15 | 1, 8 | 2, 10 |
| 6 | 1, 2, 3, 4, 5, 6, 7, 9, 10, 11, 12, 13, 16, 17, 18 | 1, 2, 5, 8, 9, 10, 12, 13, 15, 17, 18 | 9, 10 ,11, 13, 14, 15, 16, 18 | 8, 9, 12, 14 | 6 |
| 7 | 1, 2, 3, 4, 6, 7, 8, 9, 10, 13, 14, | 2, 5, 6, 7, 9, 11, 12, 16 | 2, 4, 5, 6, 7, 8, 9, 11, 13, 15, 16 | 2, 3, 5 | 4, 9, 10 |
| 8 | 1, 2, 3, 4, 6, 10, 12, 13, 14, 15, 17, 18, 20, 21 | 4, 6, 10, 12, 17, 21, 22 | 1, 4, 5, 6, 7, 8, 9, 10, 11, 12, 13, 14, 15, 16, | 16 | 8, 10, 13, 18, 19, 20, 22 |
| 9 | **S**/1, 2, 5 **H**/5, 6, 7 **G**/1, 2 **PSE**/ 1,3,4 **A**/1, 2, 3 | **S**/1, 7 **H**/1, 2, 3, 4 **A**/1, 4 **MS**/ 2, 3, 4 | **S**/1-6 **H**/1-3, 5-7 **G**/1, 3 **PS**/1, 3, 5 **A**/3, 4, 21 **MS**/1-4 | **MS**/4 | **S**/2, 5 **H**/2, 3, 4, 6 **G**/2 **PSE**/3 |
| 10 | 1, 4, 5 | 1, 3, 4, 5 | 2, 8 | 6, 7, 8 | 2, 6, 7, 8 |

# Scotland

The chart on this page refers to different components of the Scottish curriculum for English. Activities are identified by their chapter and activity numbers; for example, **2**/3 means chapter 2, Activity 3. Chapter 9 is divided into sections and these are marked accordingly with the section initial.

All the activities may be used successfully at higher levels and activities in Chapter 10 reflect the spirit of the English curriculum, but activities are too wide ranging to fit exactly into one strand or level.

| Components and strands | Levels | A | B | C | D | E |
|---|---|---|---|---|---|---|
| **Writing** | **Personal** | **1**/3,4,5,6,7,8 **3**/1,2 **4**/1,3,4 **S**/**9**/1-5 **H**/**9**/1-3 **G**/**9**/1 | **2**/3,11,13 **4**/2,3,4,9 **5**/4 **6**/11 **8**/11,13 **S**/**9**/5,6,7, | **H**/**9**/1,2,3 **P**/**9**/1,2,3 **S**/**9**/5 | **H**/**9**/7 **S**/**9**/3 | |
| | **Imaginative** | **6**/1,2,3,7 **8**/1,2,3,5 **S**/**9**/4 | **3**/4,5,6,7 **5**/6,7,8,9,10,11,12 **6**/13 **A**/**9**/1,3 **G**/**9**/2 **M**/**9**/1,2 | **3**/8,9,10,12,14,18 **5**/3,14,15,17,20 **6**/10,4/11 **S**/**9**/4,7 **H**/**9**/4 **M**/**9**/3 | **5**/9,10,11 **6**/13 **8**/8,9,12,14,16,22 **G**/**9**/3 | **M**/**9**/4 **H**/**9**/4,6 |
| | **Knowledge about language** | | **3**/7 **4**/1,8,12 **6**/8,9,12 **7**/1,11,12,13 | **3**/18 **5**/1 **6**/14,15,17 **7**/5,6,7,8,14,15 | **7**/2,4,9,10,16 **8**/20,22 | |
| **Listening** | **Listening in order to respond to texts** | **1**/9,10,11,12 **2**/3,5,6,7,12,13 **6**/4,5 **8**/1,2,3 | **7**/13 **8**/12 **H**/**9**/3,5 | **A**/**9**/4 | **H**/**9**/5 | |
| | **Awareness of genre** | **1**/1,2,4,6 **2**/1,2,3,4,5,6,8,9,10,11 **4**/5 **8**/1,2,4 | **2**/5 **7**/3 **8**/5 | **2**/5 **4**/10 **8**/3,8,9,12,13,14,15,20,21,23 | **2**/5 **8**/16,17 | **2**/5 |
| **Talking** | **Talking about texts** | **2**/2 **4**/2,5 **5**/2 **6**/4,5,6 | **1**/7 **6**/18 **8**/13 **P**/**9**/4 | **4**/8 **A**/**9**/1 **P**/**9**/4 | | |
| **Reading** | **Reading for enjoyment** | **1**/1 **2**/4,5,6 **4**/6 **5**/2 **S**/**9**/3 | **5**/8,9 **S**/**9**/3 | **S**/**9**/3 | **S**/**9**/3 | |
| | **Reading to reflect on writer's ideas and craft** | **8**/4 **2**/1,6 | **4**/10 **5**/5 **8**/4,7,10 | **4**/11 **5**/13 **6**/16 | | |

# PHOTOCOPIABLES

The pages in this section can be photocopied and adapted to suit your own needs and those of the class; they do not need to be declared in respect of any photocopying licence.

A number of these photocopiable pages relate to specific activities in the main body of the book and the appropriate activity and page references are given above the relevent sheet.

The decorative borders can be used by the children to present their poems or to brainstorm them. The children can colour them to suit their poems or add to and adapt them if they wish. They can also use them to inspire their own designs.

All about me, page 17

corative border

# Finding out

Finding out about things means that you have to look at them very closely. Here are some questions to help you look closely. Write down in the notes column what you find out and use your notes to help you in your writing.

| Questions | Notes |
|---|---|
| • What do you think it is? <br><br> • Have you seen anything like it before? Where? <br><br> • Where does it come from? How do you know? <br><br> • How old do you think it is? What tells you? <br><br> • What colour is it? <br><br> • What does the shape remind you of? <br><br> • What does it feel like? <br><br> • Does the smell or the taste remind you of anything? <br><br> • Does it make a sound? What kind of sound? <br><br> • Does it change when the sun shines on it or when it is wet? <br><br> • Does it move? How? <br><br> • What could you do with one of these things? | |

Last Will and
Testament

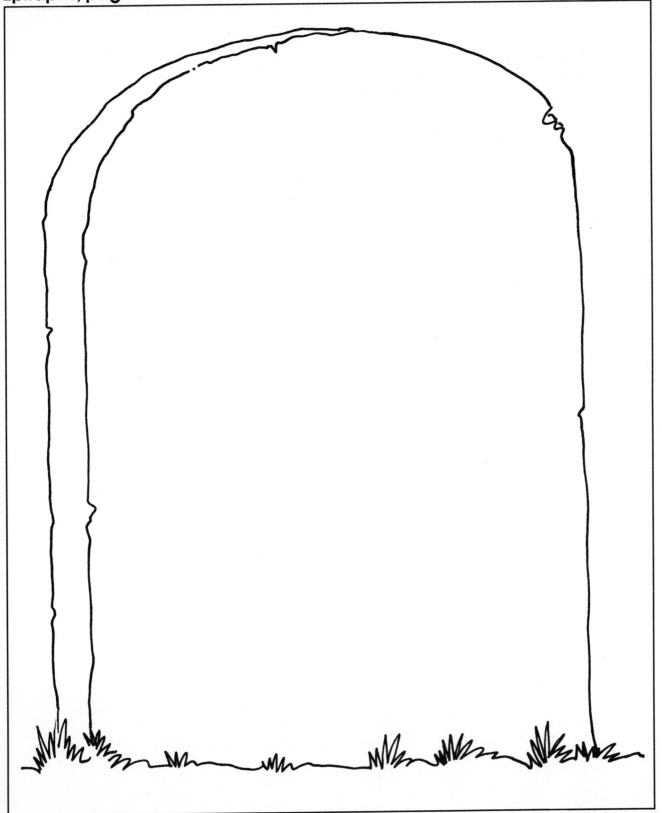

# Word heaps

Choose any five adjoining words to help you create a poem.

Autumn leaves colour red brown acorn cup saucer plate eat
drink water river sea sail boat pirate adventure treasure island
sun warm holiday sand build castle moat drawbridge soldiers
defend tanks guns fire explode heat flames flicker spread
forest alight night moon stars twinkling bright planet space
adventure alien UFO comet Hayley's circling heavens earth
dens badgers beavers trap bait catch fish food eat chips egg
sausage ketchup delicious pie blackbirds sing king queen
honey money buy rich poor none drought water rain stream
torrent rocks cascade waterfall cave secret passage
smugglers barrels tunnel channel gulls swoop fishing boat
 harbour


Problem trouble fight cut face head teacher talk punish sad
sorrow tomorrow new fresh begin again wish hope rope box
treasure buried hole tomb grave serious shake earthquake
rocks  tumble cracks split slip slide ice pond frozen water
birds skate ski snow flakes frost winter Christmas presents fun
joy tree stockings full early morning exciting flying high jet
traveller concorde beauty swan graceful hiss vicious peck
nip hurt damage accident  car motorway wide fast fog blind
touch hold feel imagine story people travel adventure brave
canoe paddle rapids dangerous rocks stone wall protect fear
home house room bed child asleep

# Christmas card competition

• Design a line drawing for a Christmas card so that it can be coloured in.

• Write a mini-poem of short seasonal verse.

• The card must be 11.5cm x 15cm and you can obtain the right size paper from your teacher.

• Put your name and class on the back of both your design and verse.

• Give your entries to _ _ _ _ _ _ _ _ _ _ _ _ _ _ _ _ _ _ _ _ _ _ _ _ _

by _ _ _ _ _ _ _ _ _ _ _ _ _ _ _ _ _ _ _ _ _ _ _ _ _ _ _ _ _ _ _ _ .

# Making a poem in ten steps

## Making a poem in ten steps

1    Choose a subject and brainstorm it to make a list of words and phrases.

2    Use the list to help you to write your poem.
     Cross out the bits you don't like.
     Add to it or alter bits, where you think you need to.

3    Read it to a friend or your table group. What do they suggest?

4    Think about those suggestions and decide whether you want to use them or not.

5    Check:
     Have you used the same descriptive word twice?
     Could you use a different one or should it be said in a different way?
     Look for repetitive phrases. Are they there for a purpose?

6    Can you think of any ways to improve the poem?

7    Check your spelling and word meanings.
     Look up any words that you are not sure of.
     Do they mean what you want them to mean?
     Have you spelt them correctly?

8    Look at the punctuation. Is it correct?

9    Copy out the poem in your very best handwriting.
     Write  it on blank paper, but put a line-guide underneath it.
     Choose which part of the page is to be written on and which part is for decoration or border.

10   Decorate your poem with care and mount your work.

     What do you think of your poem now?

# Decorative border

## Decorative border

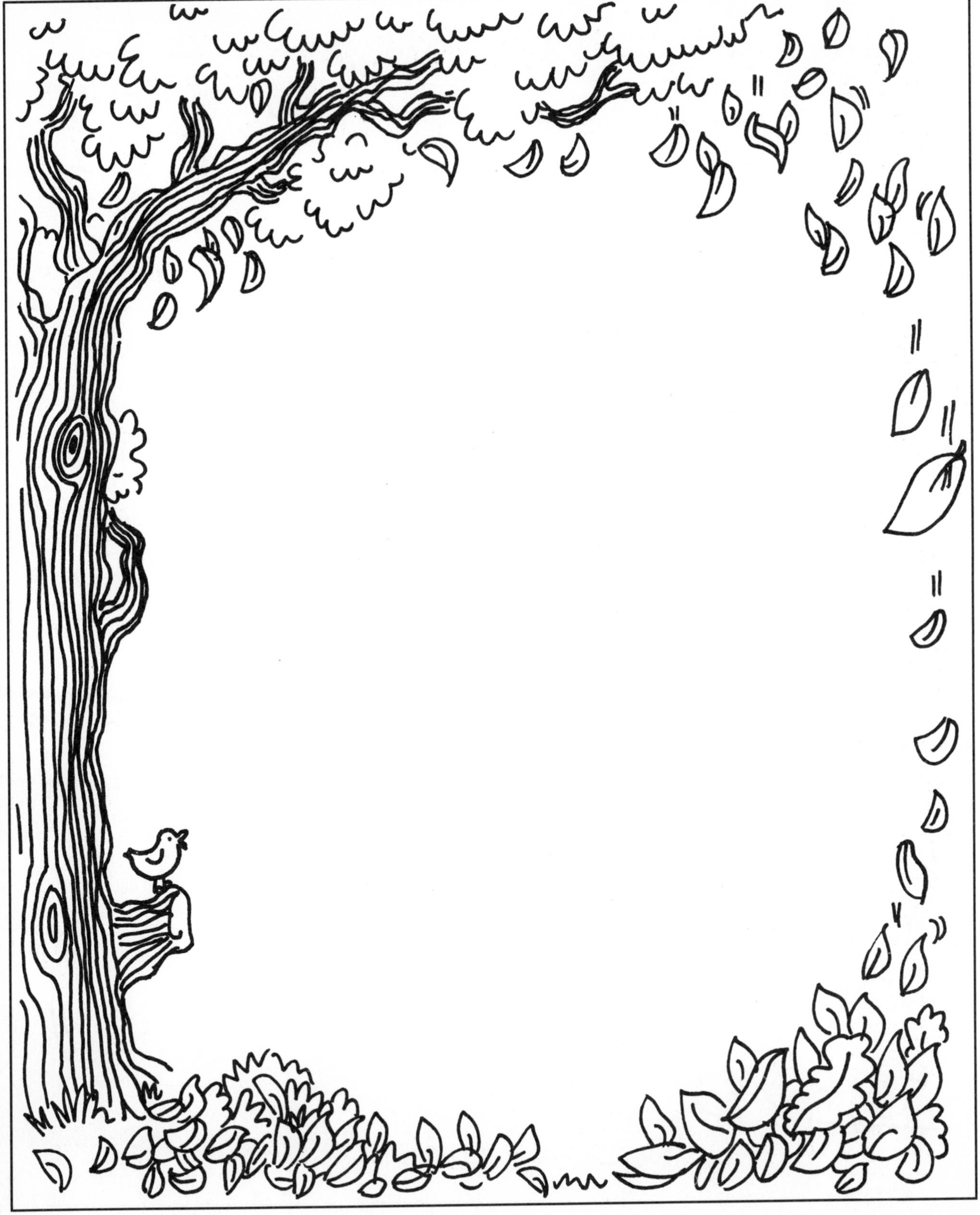

# Decorative border

# Decorative border

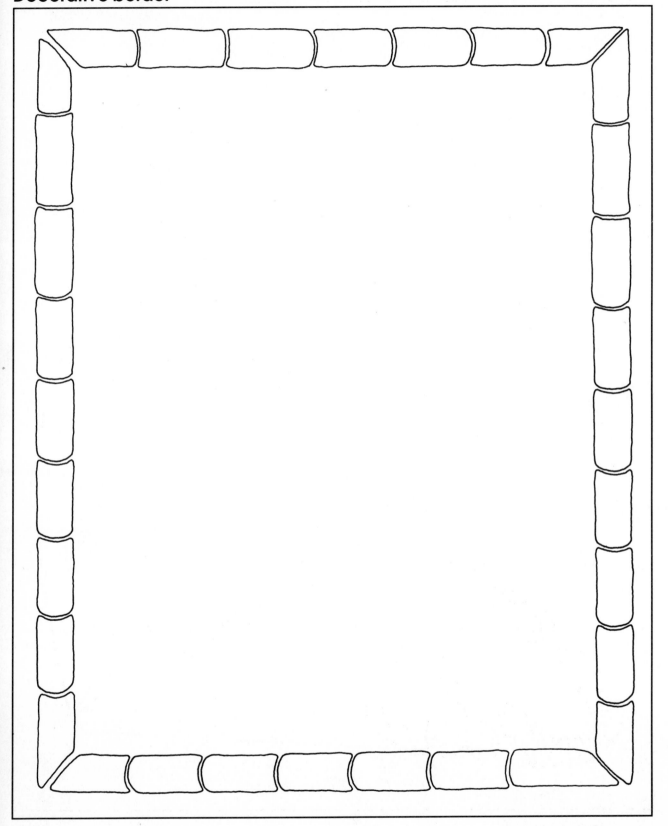

# Decorative border

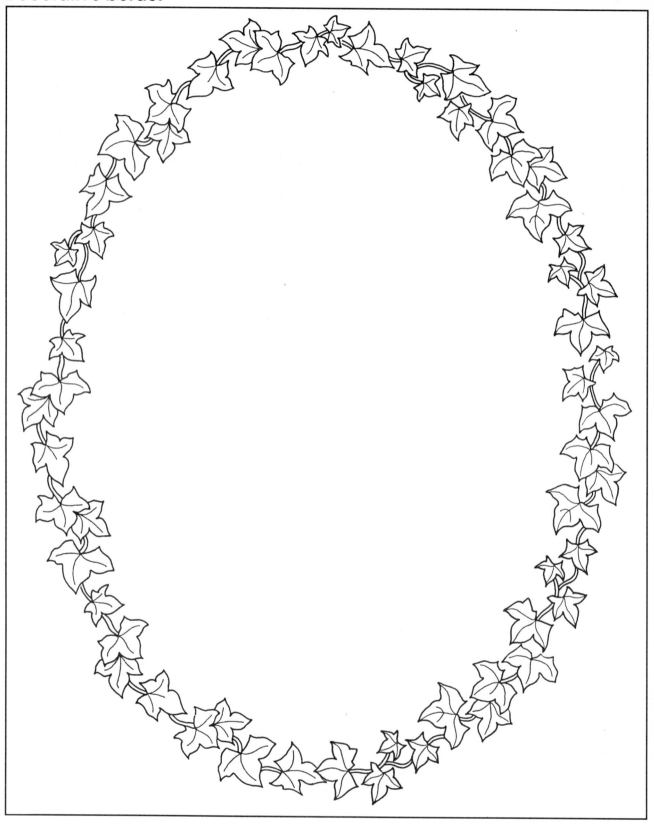